W9-AJS-358

# CHAPMAN'S LOG &

# OWNER'S MANUAL

A MOTOR BOATING & SAILING BOOK

JOHN WHITING and TOM BOTTOMLEY

HEARST BOOKS
New York, N. Y.

Published by Hearst Books
224 West 57 Street, New York, NY 10019



Library of Congress Cataloging in Publication Data
Whiting, John R
Chapman's log & owner's manual.

"A Motor boating & sailing book."
1. Boats and boating—Handbooks, manuals, etc.
I. Chapman, Charles Frederic, 1881- .
II. Bottomley, Tom, joint author. III. Title.
VM321.W44 623.8′2023 80-26191
ISBN 0-87851-801-0

**Yacht** ____________________

## GENERAL SPECIFICATIONS

Owner Name
Address ____________________ Hailing Port ____________________
City ________ State ________ Zip ________ Manufacturer ____________________
Phone (    ) ____________________ Hull Number ____________________
Club Affiliations ____________________ Registration Number ____________________
____________________ Designer ____________________
Insurance Company ____________________ Agent ____________________
____________________ Telephone ____________________

Length Overall ________ Ft. ________ m Sail Area ________ Sq. Ft. ________ $m^2$
Load Waterline Length ________ Ft. ________ m Ballast/Displacement Ratio ________
Beam ________ Ft. ________ m Sail Area/Displacement Ratio ________
Draft ________ Ft. ________ m Displacement/Load Waterline Ratio ________
Displacement ________ Lb. ________ kg Fuel Capacity ________
Ballast ________ Lb. ________ kg Water Capacity ________ Gal. ________ ltr.
Date Measured ________ Measurement Rating ________ Measuring Official ________
Bridge Clearance: Mast Height Above Water ____________________ Ft.

Engine(s) ____________________ Date Installed ____________________
Transmission(s) ____________________ Reduction Ratio ____________________
Propeller Pitch ________ Diameter ________ No. Blades ________ Material ________

Boatyard ________ Manager ________ Phone ____________________
Mechanic ________ Phone ____________________
Electronics Technician ____________________ Phone ____________________
Sailmaker ____________________ Phone ____________________
Key Numbers ____________________ Previous Owners & Dates of Ownership
____________________ ____________________ From ________ To ________
____________________ ____________________ From ________ To ________
____________________ ____________________ From ________ To ________

Radio Call Letters ____________________

# CONTENTS

MOTOR BOATING'S *Practical Series*

PRACTICAL

# *Suggestions*

## FOR HANDLING FITTING OUT AND CARING FOR *the* BOAT

VOL. VI

# INTRODUCTION

So now you own a boat. It may be your first boat or your fifth. It may be new or it may have had a previous owner who added equipment, kept everything lubricated and adjusted, and even turned over to you his handwritten notebook about adjustments, repairs and maintenance schedules. In any case, your boat is more complicated than a house, probably better made than a car—but nevertheless a mechanism with a lot of dials, adjustments, and systems to take care of.

## Mr. Chapman's Practical Suggestions

Charles F. Chapman, that redoubtable boat-owner and editor, had such strong ideas on this matter that he published a book: *Practical Suggestions for Handling, Fitting Out and Caring for The Boat.* The original cover, from 1918, appears on the facing page. Now, twenty million boats later, *you* own a boat. You probably already know that few boats come equipped with an owner's manual (but there may be a good engine manual, or good booklets about the water pressure system or the electronic communications equipment). And this book is a successor to that early book by Mr. Chapman, now brought right into the 1980's.

As the title indicates, this is both an owner's manual and a log book, for the logical reason that they belong together. You keep a record of engine oil changes, or inspections and adjustments to your electronic equipment, or parts numbers. You also keep a diary of weekend trips, or your vacation cruises, with appropriate information on courses steered, engine R.P.M., and the state of the weather. The log part of this publication is based on the original *Yacht Log Book, Guest Register and Radiotelephone Log* by Charles F. Chapman and the various improvements suggested by experienced staff members of *Motor Boating & Sailing Magazine.*

Since you probably know Mr. Chapman's most famous book, *Piloting, Seamanship & Small Boat Handling,* we need not say "doing it right is half the fun," because you already know that. However, we will add some pointers on how to use *Chapman's Log and Owners Manual.*

This is a book that is part of your boat, one of your tools. It is a double-purpose tool, with concise information about on-board maintenance and repairs in the text section, and a continuous record of trips and the work done in the log section. You may not make long trans-ocean voyages, nor need to record your position each noon from sextant sights like the captain of the clipper ship—but for the many varieties of pleasure boat usage there are special log pages. Weekend trips, parties aboard your boat, the annual vacation cruise—the diaries of recreational yachting aboard power boats and sailboats—are provided for with special sections.

## How to Use This Book

If you have a radio-telephone you are required by law to keep a record of calls, repairs and maintenance. If you keep a record of engine maintenance and repairs, you'll save money and trouble in the long run. These points are self-evident. Experience—cruising experience—has suggested other blanks to be filled in. If you have ever wracked your brain with "What was the name of that mechanic in Greenport?" you'll be glad to find space for his name and his telephone number. If some day you stand in a telephone booth at the other end of the dock, and the mechanic you are calling asks for the make and model number of a certain piece of equipment, you'll be glad you wrote it into this book, so you don't have to say "I'll go look on the nameplate and call you back."

Not every boat owner, of course, will need and use every part of this book. We do suggest you go through it, and become familiar with the contents and fill in all the applicable data. As you will note on the text pages, boldface headlines make it easy to find specific instructions in a hurry. You'll also note that this is not a book on boat handling, or navigation, or the rules of the road. It is about the mechanisms, rigging, and systems aboard a modern pleasure boat. This book relates primarily to your ownership of the boat, your insurance, and your safety insofar as the mechanical and electrical operation are concerned. For this reason an envelope is bound into the cover, to keep important "ship's papers" and booklets that come with the pump, the galley stove, the engines.

Some boat-builders and most engine builders have excellent owners' manuals for their particular products, or make up packets that include the owners' booklets for various products installed in the boat. If these booklets and leaflets are missing, try to replace them.

There are a number of other specific information sources that you may want to use. First, as most boat owners know: the U.S. Coast Guard sets certain safety standards and is charged with enforcing federal safety requirements. There are lists of required safety equipment for various sizes of boats and there are regulations about marine toilets. But two problems remain: (1) The Coast Guard does not have manpower available for complete inspections or true enforcement, and (2) In any case, the government-required equipment is a good deal less than a minimum (the requirements list navigation lights, horns, and bells, life jackets and fire extinguishers for pleasure boats—but not anchors, dock lines, pliers, flashlights, weather instruments or radios.) A new requirement, as of January 1981, is for emergency signalling devices (flares, flags, lights). It is therefore necessary for each boat owner to make his or her own safety inspection. We recommend a minimum of two careful inspections a year, plus certain procedure checks every time the boat is used.

## Items to Avoid Aboard Your Boat

We also point out: there are products that may be suitable for camping ashore that are not safe if taken on boats (portable gasoline lanterns, portable stoves and heaters.) There is no metal plate on these that says "Not for use on boats."

Similarly, many electrical switches and other devices that are perfectly suitable for home use don't last long in the dampness of the marine environment. How, then, do you tell?

On the surface, hardware sold at a marine dealer's is more likely to be right for a boat in your area than a similar item in a general hardware store. You probably already know that iron screws rust, but stainless steel and bronze screws do not. But for the wise choice of products, for installation requirements, and for proper maintenance and use instructions, you may very well turn to an authority like the American Boat and Yacht Council. This is a non-profit organization that works with the companies and individuals in the boating industry, the Coast Guard, insurance companies, and also with technical organizations such as Underwriters' Laboratories and the National Fire Protection Association. The ABYC, located in Amityville, New York, publishes *Safety Standards for Small Craft*, as well as the individual standards for scores of important technical matters (equipment such as galley stoves, engineering standards such as horse-power ratings, and hull, machinery and electrical standards).

To most boat-owners, standards that apply to "marine use" become important only when they add equipment or deal with a repairman. In a broader sense, however, it is a good idea to know something about marine engineering standards and where to get detailed information on them in situations involving purchases or sale of a boat, and insurance. Safety, economy in the long run, and the convenience of dependability can all be involved.

## Information Sources

In the text, and again in the bibliography, there are references to specific information sources. If you take a careful look at the bookshelves aboard typical boats owned by knowledgeable boatmen you will find, in addition to *Piloting, Seamanship and Small Boat Handling*, items such as marine hardware and equipment catalogs. These give the names, dimensions and other specifications of a variety of equipment, from turnbuckles to plumbing, from navigation lights and their spare bulbs to fascinating listings of special supplies like sprays for waterproofing ignition systems.

As you know from observation of other boat-owners, some rarely run into mechanical troubles and can enjoy their boating to the fullest. Others, who don't know about the regular inspection and oiling of sea-cocks, or keeping their batteries charged up, have the troubles and expenses. A few pay to have all their maintenance done—but the wisest oversee and inspect the work of even the best mechanics.

The owner's manual part of this book is for all three kinds of boat owners. It is intended to cover regular inspections and maintenance during the boating season (not overhauls), the emergency repair you can do yourself, and a program that includes the qualified expert when necessary.

## Maintenance Routine

Much of it is based on material that originally appeared in *Motor Boating & Sailing* magazine—the same magazine that Mr. Chapman edited for half a century. The Boatkeeper section in *Motor Boating & Sailing* appears almost every month, with timely articles and compact information on boat maintenance.

There are other echoes of experience here too: cruising logs maintained over twenty-five years aboard *Merrywend I, II* and *III;* advice from Lou Grill who was long the technical manager for Universal Motors; conversations at the famous City Island Yacht Club with Eddie Quest who ran the yard and had earlier sailed in square riggers; a "Defect Book" idea—notes on a brand new boat in a composition book—from the London boat show; pointers on rigging care from Sam Barclay at Stamford's Yacht Haven; and guidance on routine inspections from Carleton Mitchell, whose *Finisterre* thrice won the Bermuda Race. Experience and observations as chairman of many offshore power boat races is a part of the editors' personal background. Much of the technical material in this book, of course, is from The Boatkeeper section of *Motor Boating & Sailing* magazine, with the cooperation of the editor, Oliver Moore, and of the publisher, Robert O'Connor. E.S. Maloney, noted for his authorship of most of the recent editions of *Piloting*, gave freely of his advice on this book too.

The authors thank the various contributors whose material has been excerpted—and also William Bossert, who made important contributions to the typographical design of this book, as well as Jennifer Coleman, whose drawing of an outboard cruiser graces the Children's Log pages.

As for Mr. Chapman's Log . . . at the beginning of the Log Pages there is a short section, part of it as originally written by Mr. Chapman, on keeping a log. *—John R. Whiting/Thomas R. Bottomley*

# TOOLS/SPARES

When our great-grandfathers were sailing in schooners or square-riggers, every seaman carried a knife. It was the basic tool. Fids, sailor's palms, and sailmaker's needles were the other essential personal tools.

## Work Bench

Today, even the smallest boat, out for a short run, should have a knife, a screw-driver and probably a pair of vise-grip pliers aboard. At the other end of the scale, a well-found larger cruising boat might very well have a small workbench, compound-lever bolt cutters and even a battery-operated quarter-inch drill aboard. The use to which a boat will be put—and where—should govern the selection of tools.

In this chapter we will take a look at tools and spares, their storage and care, remembering that we are talking about routine on-board maintenance and the handling of a variety of problem-solving situations. (The tools in your complete home workshop, or the ones you need for spring fitting out, are another subject.)

Not everyone has discovered the joys of working with good quality and suitable tools. But almost everyone has tried to cope with a mechanical problem where the equipment was wrong or the knowledge was a trifle inadequate. So, for a few paragraphs, let us take a fresh look at some basics. If you already know these things . . . use these points as a reminder for your less knowledgeable brother-in-law.

## Seven Pointers

1. Fine quality tools, of good steel or other material that's suitable, are worth the extra cost—not just eventually, but by the second time you use them.

2. You can make a small toolbox a good one by choosing in advance the tools that fit your potential problems or specific situations. A long-bladed screwdriver for an otherwise inaccessible hose clamp. One large open-end wrench that fits the nut on your stuffing box. A gimlet, because on this vacation cruise you plan to install some small item with wood screws.

3. To keep seldom-used metal tools rust-free, spray them with silicone or Teflon spray and put them in clear plastic bags—the common kitchen

type with twistems, or zip-lock bags. Light oil, vaseline, or spray oil also work, of course.

4. If you're the kind of boat-owner who likes to occasionally repair a worn bit or varnish or paint, there are two ways to avoid the mess and work of cleaning the brush afterward. (a) Carry a couple of small inexpensive throw-away brushes. (b) Secure an empty container that has the brush built into the lid. Some rubber cement cans and bottles qualify. Put your varnish or paint in the can, and close it tightly. You can also make a brush-top lid by cutting a hole in the lid and sealing the brush in place with automotive windshield sealer, epoxy putty or silicone rubber sealer. (As you can see, in this chapter we are taking a broader view of "tools" than merely pliers and wrenches.)

5. Some small squares of sandpaper and emery cloth, a plastic box with an assortment of suitable screws, bolts and cotter pins, and a spray can of Teflon lubricant, CRC or WD-40 don't add up to a lot of volume in your tool drawer. The choice of such items depends on how long a cruise you're making, how far you expect to be from marine dealers, and your own boat.

6. To sharpen a knife (including a galley knife or two) include a small carborundum stone or a file in your basics.

7. Sometimes you have to adapt a tool or even make one. Your file can be used to dress a screw-driver (that's the technical term for keeping it square at the tip) and also to make it a little smaller to fit a special screw head. A pair of small Vise-Grips can be clamped on a short screwdriver to improvise an angle screwdriver and get extra leverage.

## Tool Box

Now let us look at the ideal complete tool chest for a cruising boat.

**Knives.** Almost every boatman carries at least a pocket knife. Sailboat owners are well advised to carry a rigging knife, such as the Ka-Bar. The small locking fid is useful for splicing. Usually there is a strong steel U-shaped shackle—which is best for opening rigging shackles. The fid can be used for this too, but it's sharp and not usually as good. The other use for the shackle on the knife, of course, is to enable its use with a lanyard that fastens on your belt. About 18 inches is a convenient lanyard length. The knife is usually kept in your pocket, but the lanyard prevents accidental loss. Another excellent knife to have aboard is an electrician's knife. It's surprising that more aren't seen, because the screwdriver second blade is a great convenience.

## Screwdrivers

**Screwdrivers.** Don't try to use a screwdriver as a chisel, but otherwise it's one of the most-used tools. Choosing which ones you need, of course, depends on the various places you may have to work. A very short screwdriver is sometimes needed in a very tight space. A long one will reach where your hand won't fit. A large diameter handle, as you know, gives you extra turning power. Usually two or three sizes of blade are sufficient. One or more Phillips-head screwdrivers are needed on most boats. Some engine parts, some electronic equipment housings, and some appliances have Phillips-head screws. A handy special tool is an offset or angle screwdriver. Some come with standard slot type drivers at different angles on each end, so you can make small turns in difficult places. Another kind has a standard slot type driver at one end, and a Phillips-head at the other. Ordinarily, ratchet or automatic screwdrivers, and those with screw-holding attachments are more likely to be used on major installation projects and don't need to live aboard. Allen-wrench types, usually in a set of several sizes, are sometimes needed for set screws and other special situations.

**Tool Locker**

**Pliers**

**Pliers.** The commonest pliers are called slip-joint pliers. They are used a lot, and are quick, but they have disadvantages. When used on a nut, if they are not held in an iron-strong fist, they can chew up the nut. (Use a wrench of the proper size.) Much better for most purposes are Vise-Grip pliers, which have a compound lever system, lock in place, and are truly engineered for good work. These come with square-faced jaws and rounded jaws, in a variety of sizes. There'll be times when you'll use one as a vise to hold work. Electricians' pliers, long nose pliers and even tweezers are good to have aboard if you have space.

**Wrenches**

**Wrenches.** The beginner with tools makes a great discovery early on. The monkey wrench. Later on he discovers that an adjustable wrench or two, although useful, is not nearly as good for engine work as a socket wrench, an open-end wrench, or a box wrench. (One space saving method is to get a set of combination wrenches . . . box wrench on one end, open-end on the other.) A new problem in wrenches, that will be around for a long, long time, is that more and more equipment requires metric sizes—and the inch measurement nuts and bolts are still around. At times you can use one type of wrench on the other size of nut—it almost fits. So if your mechanical items are in two types of measurement systems, you'd best consider having two sets of wrenches if you're voyaging under conditions where you may have to make extensive repairs. (For many size situations, the versatile Vise-Grip pliers will do. At least they're adjustable.)

**Hacksaw.** This is one tool you probably will not use often, and a good substitute that takes up small space is just a hacksaw blade or two. When using a hacksaw to cut metal, make a small start with a file first. Makes it easier.

**Hammers.** A hammer is rarely used abord a boat—but if you're used to tools you may well ask, "But what if I *need* a hammer?" The answer is

**Hammers** (a) You probably won't be driving nails. (b) For a small tap or two, use the back of a wrench. (c) If you may occasionally be going ashore and organizing a cookout fire on the beach, you'll find a scout axe handy for splitting firewood . . . and the back of a scout axe makes a fair to middling hammer. (d) If you are going to have a complete tool box, get a small machinist's hammer before you get a carpenter's hammer.

**Files** **Files.** A small flat file, and a small triangular file, kept clean and rust-free, are useful tools that take up little space. A file will sharpen a knife, dress a rounded screw driver so it works efficiently, or cut off a bronze bolt.

**Oil Can/Sprays.** When you make your weekly check of the engine, or your monthly check of the seacocks, you need an oil can. A standard steel oil can will do, but it will eventually rust. A brass oil can is better. One with a pressure plunger is most convenient. A spray can of lubricant . . . with Teflon or the penetrating type like CRC or WD-40 has many uses. One extra use, for damp-proofing ignition wires, is discussed in the chapter on engines. For more on sprays, see the end of this chapter.

**Fid.** Not just for sailors, the fid is a good tool. If you occasionally make a splice, you may well want a fid. With small line that's fairly soft and flexible, your fingers will do. Under a lot of other conditions, one or more fids will come in handy and result in better rope work. If you are going to be splicing braided line, you almost *have* to have a special hollow fid. For an all-purpose fid, get the one manufactured by Fid-O. It's light, can't rust, and it has a push-through design that really works. Several sizes are available. Made by Fido-O/McGrew Splicing Tool Co., 8120 Rio Linda Blvd., Elverto, California 95626.

**Palm and Needle.** If you may have to repair a sail or awning, a sailor's palm, sailmaker's needles, and sail twine are needed. Useful also for rope work, like serving the end of a line. Several sizes of twine are good. Sailors and powerboatmen alike are now and then surprised to find a sailmaker's palm aboard a power cruiser. Truly, it's an excellent tool for working on dock lines, dinghy painters, awnings. Another useful item that comes in a can is Whip-End Dip. It's a quick sealer for rope ends, marking anchor lines and sealing in splices. It's sold by Marine Development & Research Corp., 115 Church Street, Freeport, N.Y. 11520, and like most of this company's useful products, is generally available at marine dealers.

**Grommet Punch and Die.** If you plan to repair or alter an awning, make a canvas tool bag or a set of curtains, a grommet punch and die, plus blank brass grommets, is an interesting and useful tool. Easy to learn to use.

**Spark plug wrench.** This is a special tool; make sure it fits your spark plugs. (If you have an outboard or a generator motor, the plugs are probably a different size. You need two wrenches.) Advantage: gets at the plug in a difficult spot, doesn't harm the plug as an adjustable or open end wrench might.

## Abrasives

**Scotch-brite.** In the household size or in a larger industrial or shop size, this abrasive is a very useful extra to have aboard. Cleans, even gives you the equivalent of very light sanding. However, on brass or bronze it will dull a bright finish.

**Electrical.** Electrical tape, the vinyl kind, and possibly a small piece of spare wire, would be included in the spares and supplies. Electrical tape and sail repair tape are also useful in non-electrical and non-sail emergencies. A hydrometer is valuable.

**Hand Drill and Bits.** Useful now and then, a small hand drill—probably the type with a rotating crank-wheel rather than the standard carpenter's brace—plus a clear plastic box with an assortment of drills, is something you undoubtedly need for home repairs, for fall or spring work on the boat, and in some cases you might include this equipment on a cruising boat. If all you plan to do is install one small bronze coat hook for your foul weather gear, a gimlet will do.

**Ignition Tools.** In the chapter on engines, it is suggested that a complete set of spares for your engine or engines be included. Similarly, a small kit of ignition tools, with gauges, small pliers, and perhaps test lamps is a good thing to know about.

**Plumbing tools.** The tools already described, particularly Vise-Grip pliers in two or three sizes, will take care of most plumbing situations on a boat. Rarely, if your piping calls for it, you might have need of a Stillson wrench. Such a pipe wrench will turn a round pipe, as in an engine cooling installation, where most other tools won't work.

**Electrical Spares and Supplies.** Unless you're planning a specific project during a long cruise, like installing an extra circuit, the basic tools already listed will do. You don't need a great deal more—but if you're going to be far away from marine supply houses, a few feet of wire, some spare light bulbs (both cabin lights and running lights) and of course spare fuses are sensible to have aboard. These items take up little room and if they're properly stowed they don't deteriorate. It's a rare boat that would have a soldering iron in the tool box.

## Spare Parts

**Other Spare Parts.** Extra turnbuckles, toggles, thimbles, spare line, small pieces of canvas for chafing gear—all these get on a list for extended cruising, depending on the boat and the areas to be cruised. Pump impellers, gaskets, washers . . . these items may never be needed, or they may be needed very much. Spare parts for the intricate marine toilet are often a must.

# TOOLS/SPARES

**Items in Tubes and Spray Cans.** The inventiveness of man has been very good for the boat-owner. Silicone rubber, usually in tubes, seals small deck leaks. Vinyl cleaner (Loco is one brand) is a useful special product. Note: stove alcohol, on sponge, rag, or paper towel, will clean plastic-covered lifelines. Various foaming fiberglass cleaners save work if you like to keep the upper works of your boat shining. There are good cleaners for clear plastic, and you may even want to have a plastic scratch remover.

## Spray Coatings

**An Ounce of Prevention.** One of the useful and most frequently reached-for "tools" in every professional mechanic's toolbox is really not a tool at all. It is a can of multi-purpose, moisture-displacing penetrating lubricant that is also widely used as a protective coating for combating oxidation on all kinds of metal surfaces, as well as in all types of electrical equipment. Available in most marine outlets, as well as in practically all auto supply and hardware stores, these versatile "liquid problem solvers" are light-bodied, low-viscosity, clear liquid lubricants that have two unusual qualities which set them apart from ordinary lubricating oils:

First, they have exceptional penetrating power and will seep into microscopic crevices and tight fitting joints, even when the parts involved are covered with caked-on rust. Second, they will quickly displace water and other foreign materials and will then form a coating that will keep moisture from working its way in—all this without interfering with the transmission of electric currents, even when used on terminals or inside electrical sockets.

It is this second characteristic—the ability to displace moisture and coat surfaces with a moisture-repellent film—that has made these products useful to anyone who works on mechanical or electrical equipment in a marine environment.

Usually packaged in aerosol cans (they are also available in bulk containers for large-volume users), these versatile lubricant/coatings are made by many companies who package them under various brand names—although WD-40, LPS and CRC are probably the three best-known.

**Hard-to-Find Tools.** Many specialized tools are not offered by standard hardware, marine supply, or building supply stores. For a catalog displaying such hard-to-find items, write to Brookstone Company, 118 Brookstone Bldg., Peterborough, NH 03458.

Except for work on deck or with rigging, there are two special problems that come up when you are doing most kinds of maintenance or repairs aboard a boat: the spaces around motors, drive shafts, and plumbing are almost always very tight and often dark.

If your boat did not come with a light in the engine compartment, installing one is fairly simple. A flashlight is not nearly so handy—but can be made more so if you put in a strategically located hook or two from which to hang it. Many boats carry a trouble light—either the standard kind with a 12-volt bulb substituted for the 115-120 volt bulb, or the smaller automotive type, which usually plugs into a cigarette lighter accessory outlet. These outlets are easily obtained and installed.

## Flashlight Bracket

More on flashlights: find a couple of non-rusting brackets to hold a flashlight, and install them just inside a lazarette hatch, or on the inside of the hatch itself, and you'll have an easy-access flashlight for the occasional hurry-up times when you can't go below. Another handy place for a set of flashlight brackets is on the underside of a dinghy thwart.

On some boats you'll find a small shelf installed for an oil can, near the motor. A one-opening replica of the wooden holders for liquor bottles often found in the galley will do nicely.

In addition to tools, a lot of other items seem to end up in the tool locker as well. A piece of canvas or tarpaulin, for instance, can be spread out in the cockpit or on the ground in a boatyard, to keep a greasy pump you're working on from dirtying the deck, or mud from caking on good tools. Here are other items that are useful.

**Non-Tools for Your Tool Box**

Magnet • Pocket Flashlight • Tape • Whipping Thread • Rags • Plastic Drop Cloth • Monel Wire • Rigger's Apron • Roll of Paper Towels • Staple Gun & Monel Staples • Can of Bedding & Sealing Compound • Epoxy Putty & Glue • Marline • Stainless Steel Cotter Rings & Pins • Stainless Shackles & Hose Clamps • Current Checker & Continuity Tester • Pencils • Pad • Tape Measure

Other information on tools is to be found in the section on Rigging and that on Propulsion.

# PRE-START CHECK LIST

Indicate here all items to be checked before engine start-up.

Date Checked

Bilges ______________________________

Ground Tackle ______________________________

Life Preservers ______________________________

Horn Operation ______________________________

Navigation Lights ______________________________

Fire Extinguishers ______________________________

Mooring Lights ______________________________

Fenders ______________________________

Water ______________________________

Stove Fuel ______________________________

Flashlight ______________________________

Binoculars ______________________________

Navigation Tools ______________________________

Charts ______________________________

Electronic Equipment ______________________________

______________________________

Sails ______________________________

Rigging ______________________________

Weather Forecast ______________________________

Master Switch ______________________________

# WHEN YOU STEP ABOARD

If you're like most average boat-owners, the first time you look over the pre-start check-list shown on the opposite page, you may very well say "Who, me? Do all that?"

So let's take the pre-start check-list idea and look at it from several angles. If you've gone fishing, or cruising or sailing with a truly knowledgeable boatowner, and if you've been observant, here's what you've seen: On the dock, or coming up to his boat in a launch or dinghy, the boatowner starts looking automatically. Is a dock line chafed? Or is some rigging aloft flapping? Is anything out of place or broken?

As he steps aboard, he is not smoking, and he is likely to ask any guests not to smoke until the hatches have been opened, the blower run, and the boat aired out. There *could* be fumes from a fuel leak. In any event, he looks, listens, and smells as he first comes aboard.

Most owners can tell by the feel of the boat if there's a lot of water in the bilge. But even with boats that never seem to leak, they check the bilges . . . either by looking or by operating the bilge pump.

The master switch is turned on. If the boat is likely to be used at night the navigation lights are turned on and off, as a check to make sure they're all working.

If the horn is electric, the time to check it is early, not when one has to sound a warning signal.

Most of the other items on the check list are checked visually as one goes about stowing contents of boatbags and duffle bags.

**Seacocks**

If it is the owner's practice to close seacocks when leaving the boat, now it the time to open the ones involved with engine cooling water intake. (Seacocks for the head and galley, and sometimes for the cockpit scuppers can be opened now or later, of course.)

If you're about to go on a two week vacation, the topped-off water tanks and fuel tanks are on the check list. If you're going out for an afternoon, a check of the gauges and remembering "we filled the water tank only a week ago" is usually adequate.

## WHEN YOU STEP ABOARD

That's one part of an approach to the check list. But if you're new to boating, or there are a lot of equipment items, a written check-off is more useful than it is bothersome. Watch a good private airplane pilot or a professional airman use such a list before he takes off, and you may feel more at home with the idea.

A lot depends on the type of boat. When you start engine or engines, there's not as much to look for if you have only one or two instruments. Most people wait a couple of minutes, then check that the oil pressure is up, the ammeter registers charge, and that the cooling water is being discharged in the normal way. Most check that the main battery switch is set to charge the starting battery first, and then later switched over to the battery used for lighting.

As you look at the engine check-list, you may see an item or two that doesn't apply to your boat. You may see an item that you learn from experience needs checking only once a month. A comparison with the engine owner's manual may help in perfecting this list.

The engine instruments check list can have the same comment—not everyone has the same full range of dials. But the "normal" range for various dials is something to either memorize or write down.

Here's a difference worth noting. Your boat instruments panel may or may not have warning or so-called idiot lights like a car . . . but it is much more common to look at the instruments every twenty minutes or so aboard a boat (similarly in piloting an airplane).

In addition to the operating routines given in this section, you will find certain other maintenance check lists under Plumbing, Engine, Propulsion System, and a couple of other places in this book . . . each with a schedule to be made up in accordance with the appropriate manufacturer's recommendations.

### Starting Instructions

Write in here the starting procedures for your engine(s), or paste in photocopies of this information from your engine owner's manual. Indicate procedures for both a cold engine and a hot engine.

________________________________________

________________________________________

________________________________________

________________________________________

# WHEN YOU STEP ABOARD

INSTRUMENTS
Indicate here instrument readings at normal cruising speed. Any significant variation in readings may indicate engine malfunctions.

**Instruments**

| | Port Engine | Starboard Engine |
|---|---|---|
| Tachometer | __________ | __________ |
| Water Temperature | __________ | __________ |
| Oil Pressure | __________ | __________ |
| Oil Temperature | __________ | __________ |
| Exhaust Temperature | __________ | __________ |
| Ammeter | __________ | __________ |
| Voltmeter | __________ | __________ |
| Transmission Oil Press. | __________ | __________ |
| Transmission Oil Temp. | __________ | __________ |
| Other | __________ | __________ |
| __________ | __________ | __________ |
| __________ | __________ | __________ |
| __________ | __________ | __________ |

| ENGINE | Dates Checked |
|---|---|
| Oil Level | |
| Transmission Oil Level | |
| Coolant | |
| Fuel Supply | |
| Controls Operation | |
| Generator Oil Level | |
| Batteries | |

Note: Date columns are double—so you can make a second check mark if yours is a twin-engine boat.

At the end of a run, there's another normal set of procedures. If you're leaving the boat, there are other steps. The check-list provided here is an all-purpose one. Modify it to fit your boat.

# WHEN YOU STEP ABOARD

## Speed Curve

There are two extremely useful types of information that can be plotted as curves on a graph; the first is a *speed* curve; the other is a *fuel consumption curve.* These are not often used in conjunction with auxiliary sailboat operation, but if yours is a powerboat, they are almost essential for good cruise planning and piloting.

Since few powerboats are fitted with speedometers (although reasonably accurate models are becoming available), speed is plotted against engine rpm, and the information obtained is extremely accurate as long as there are no major changes in conditions (boat loading, bottom fouling).

To develop a speed curve, make runs over a known distance at engine speeds of 500, 1,000, or 2,000 rpm intervals—whatever will give you a number of plotted points over your engine's operating range. Time the run in one direction, then reverse course, and without changing rpm, time the run in the opposite direction. Figure the speed for each direction, then average the two speeds to obtain actual speed through the water. You'll get incorrect results if you total the time for the two runs, then determine speed for the total time and distance. By making a run in both directions at each engine speed, you cancel out any current effects.

To find speed, multiply distance by 60, and divide the result by the time for a run, in minutes. Here's an example: Distance of the run is 1.8 miles, and a run in one direction requires 8.7 minutes; the run in the opposite direction takes only 7.6 minutes. Speed for the first run is:

$$\frac{1.8 \times 60}{8.7} = \frac{108}{8.7} = 12.4 \text{ knots}$$

Speed for the second run is:

$$\frac{108}{7.6} = 14.2 \text{ knots}$$

Add the two speeds and divide by two:

$$\begin{array}{l} 12.4 \\ \underline{14.2} \\ \dfrac{26.6}{2} = 13.3 \text{ knots} \end{array}$$

Speed through the water at that particular engine setting is 13.3 knots. (If you measure distance in statute miles, your speed will be statute miles per hour.)

## Fuel Consumption Curve

If possible, establish a fuel flow curve based on engine speed. A fuel flow meter is a useful tool for this, or the rates can be established after each of a series of runs at various engine speeds. The runs should be long enough—at least one hour—to provide significant indications, taking into account slow speed operation in the vicinity of the fuel dock. At a minimum, you should determine how many running hours you have, running on one tank, at a reasonable speed.

Both speed and fuel consumption curves should be plotted with the boat carrying a normal load. Keep in mind that heavier or lighter loads, boat trim, severe sea and weather conditions, and accumulations of marine growth on the bottom will affect both speed and fuel consumption.

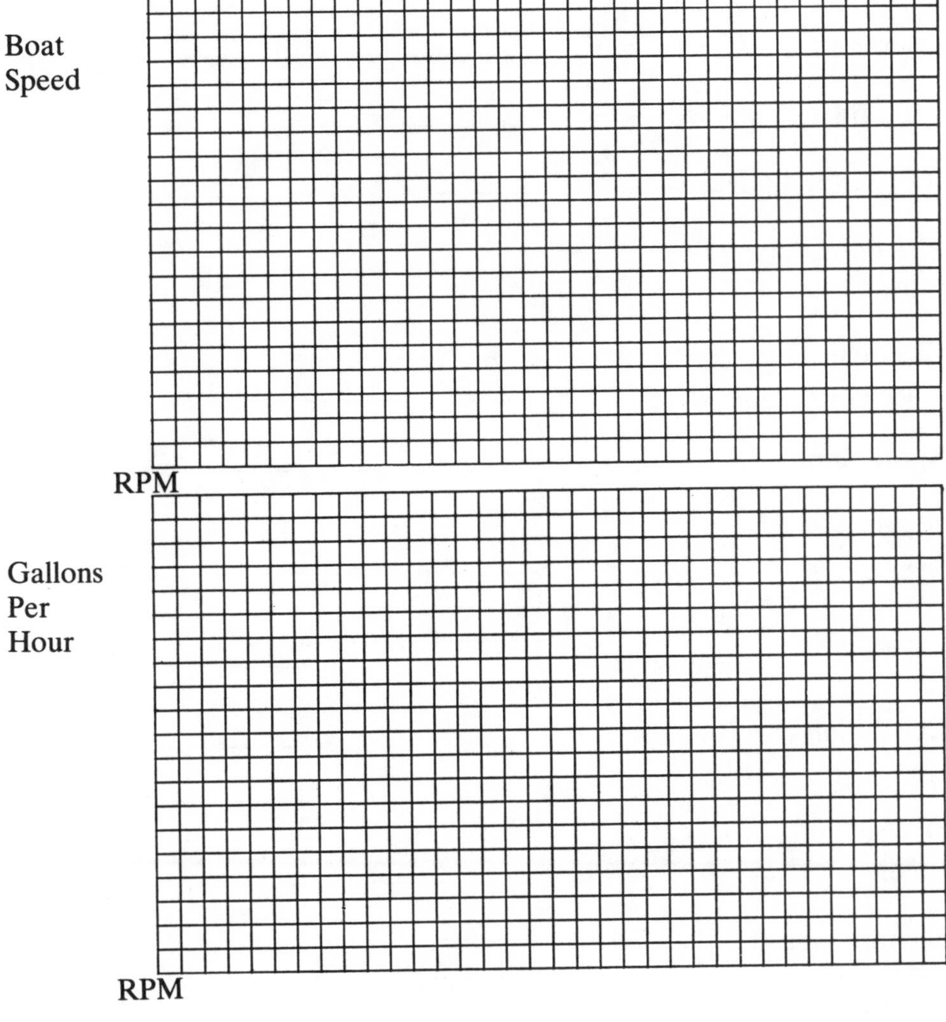

# WHEN YOU STEP ABOARD

## Shut-Down Checklist

| | Dates Checked |
|---|---|
| Engine(s) stopped | |
| Anchor Secure | |
| Mooring Lines Secure | |
| Galley Fire Out | |
| LPG tank valve off | |
| Perishables Removed from Galley | |
| Auto Bilge Pump Set | |
| Ice Chest Emptied | |
| Life Preservers Stowed | |
| Electronic Gear Unshipped | |
| Master Switch Off | |
| Rigging, Sails Secured | |
| | |
| Ventilation Okay | |
| Hatches, Windows Secured | |
| Security System Activated | |

# HULL/DECK/CABIN

You may be one who has the boatyard do all the normal maintenance to hull, deck and interior; off-season layup, painting, and the dozens of pre-launching chores. Or you may have three stalwart offspring and do almost all the work as a family. Or, like most boat-owners, your schedule of owner-managed maintenance may be somewhere in between these two approaches. In any case, the prudent boat owner specifies what is to be done, keeps appropriate records, and does enough inspecting and checking to make sure that all is well.

Detailed instructions for the year-round maintenance procedures and major projects are beyond the scope of this book. Necessary records and check lists, particularly for launching and haul-out, are included. The special checklist for sailboats is by the noted naval architect and sailor, Rod Stephens. It happens to include items beyond hull, deck and cabin. (See also Stephens' section on the proper and safe way to go aloft for repairs, using a bo's'n's chair, in the Rigging/Hardware chapter.) The check list for power boats in this chapter, by Jack Haigh, service manager of Connecticut's Norwalk Cove Marina, is also an over-all check-list. Many sailboat owners will find it useful.

## Paints and Finishes

For best results, paint or finish systems should be based on compatible products from the same paint manufacturer. List here the sealers, fillers, undercoats, primers, finish coats, and anti-fouling paints used. For new boats, this information may be in the owner's manual, or it can be supplied by the manufacturer. Even though this information does not often relate to on-board maintenance, it is a desirable part of the basic record.

**Gel Coats:** Indicate gel coat colors as specified by the boat manufacturer, and sources of matching color kits for gel coat repairs.

________________________________________

________________________________________

________________________________________

# HULL/DECK/CABIN

**Hull Bottom:**

| Material | Brand | Color | Quantity Required | Dates of Application |
|---|---|---|---|---|
| Sealer | | | | |
| Primer | | | | |
| Undercoat | | | | |
| Anti-Fouling | | | | |

**Hull Topsides:**

| Material | Brand | Color | Quantity Required | Dates of Application |
|---|---|---|---|---|
| Sealer | | | | |
| Primer | | | | |
| Undercoat | | | | |
| Finish Coat | | | | |

**Bootstripe:**

| Material | Brand | Color | Quantity Required | Dates of Application |
|---|---|---|---|---|
| Finish Coat | | | | |

**Decks:**

Sealer ______________________________

Primer ______________________________

Undercoat ______________________________

Finish Coat ______________________________

# HULL/DECK/CABIN

| Material | Brand | Color | Quantity Required | Dates of Application |
|---|---|---|---|---|

**Superstructure:**

Sealer ________________________________________

Primer ________________________________________

Undercoat ______________________________________

______________________________________________

______________________________________________

Finish Coat _____________________________________

______________________________________________

**Spars:**

Sealer ________________________________________

Primer ________________________________________

Undercoat ______________________________________

Finish Coat _____________________________________

**Interior:**

Sealer ________________________________________

Primer ________________________________________

Undercoat ______________________________________

______________________________________________

______________________________________________

Finish Coat _____________________________________

______________________________________________

# HULL/DECK/CABIN

**Engine:**
Primer ______________________________

Finish Coat ______________________________

**Brightwork:**
Sealer ______________________________

Stain ______________________________

Varnish ______________________________

List here all drains and seacocks to be opened when the boat is hauled.

| Drain | Location | Dates Drained |
|---|---|---|
| | | |
| | | |
| | | |

If your boat is stored in the north, include low point of water supply lines and all other water drainage points needed to prevent freezing damage.

List here all drains and seacocks that must be closed before the boat is launched.

| Drain | Location | Dates Closed |
|---|---|---|
| | | |
| | | |
| | | |

List here sacrificial zinc anodes used to provide protection against galvanic and cathodic corrosion.

| Zinc | Location | Dates Replaced |
|---|---|---|
| | | |

# HULL/DECK/CABIN

## Rod Stephens' Pre-Float Checklist: Sail

Ever since the yawl *Dorade* won a trans-Atlantic race in 1932 the name of Rod Stephens has been synonymous for "sailor," as Sparkman and Stephens has meant "naval architects." Rod Stephens' uncanny eye inspects boats under construction, boats before races, and boats just passing. He has learned what might go wrong and what should be right *before* going to sea. He has a special clarity in the way he points out the details of these matters. Following is his personal pre-float checklist for sailboats. Half a century of experience, as a professional naval architect and an amateur who loves sailing, is the basis for this working set of instructions, applicable to almost any size or type of sailing craft.

**HULL**

☐ Paint in good condition, even behind cradle supports.

☐ Folding or feathering prop free and lubricated. Securely attached to shaft.

☐ Speedometer transducer correctly aligned.

☐ Centerboard (if applicable) clean, smooth, operating freely. Red marks on pennant at full-up and full-down positions. Green marks: one for ¼, two for ½, three for ¾-down positions.

☐ Rudder turns freely, but with no lost motion between blade and rudder stock.

**DECK**

☐ Nonskid surface in good condition.

☐ Winches lubricated. Spare springs, pawls and necessary tools on board. Winch handle holders installed where needed.

☐ Compass aligned (with *no* internal correctors on sailboats).

☐ Elkhide on wheel rim. King spoke clearly marked. Quadrant with precise mark indicating when rudder is exactly straight. (To facilitate precise in-water adjustment of king spoke. If tiller, it should be precisely aligned with rudder.)

☐ Life raft inspection certificate obtained. Raft securely stowed but easily available.

☐ Life rings and man-overboard markers in place. Water lights working.

☐ Storm covers aboard for all hatches forward of the cockpit.

☐ Genoa sheet tracks numberd on every 5th location hole. (A waterproof marking pen can be used.)

☐ All chocks (dinghy, spinnaker poles, boat hook, reaching strut, anchor), secure.

☐ Life lines set tight. Bow and stern pulpits and stanchions secure. Toggles *(not* nylon ones) on all end attachments.

☐ Emergency boarding (at stern) provided—or a swimming ladder.

☐ Fenders, fender boards and four dock lines stowed.

**Rod Stephens' Pre-Float Checklist: Sail**

# HULL/DECK/CABIN

## CABIN

- ☐ Sea cocks lubricated with waterpump grease. Marked for purpose, and for "open" and "closed" positions.
- ☐ Bilge cleaned. Limber holes clear. Internal ballast clean and secure.
- ☐ Bilge pumps tested. Intake screens clean. Spares for pumps on board.

Floor boards not too tight (a 10° under-bevel is a good idea).

- ☐ All doors and drawers free. Latches working.
- ☐ Stove valves marked for "on" and "off" positions. Flexible feed line in good condition. Stove holds pressure (if applicable), and has insulation over it on the under deck.
- ☐ Water tanks clean and supply pumps working. High-grade check valves installed in lowest part of supply lines leading to pumps.

## MECHANICAL/ELECTRICAL

- ☐ Emergency tiller stowed with tools for installation. Spare chain and cable assembly on board.
- ☐ Tools clean and lubricated.
- ☐ Propeller shaft has double matching marks showing fixed or feathered propeller vertical, or folding propeller horizontal. Simple and effective shaft lock available (spare pins if sheer pin type).
- ☐ Oil level in gear box okay.
- ☐ Pot drained (if water-lock exhaust).
- ☐ Shaft moves freely, without excess bearing clearance.
- ☐ Batteries clean, filled to the right level with distilled water, fully charged and well-secured.
- ☐ Lightning grounding properly installed, from metal spar and from top shrouds and stays to ground plate (if ballast internal) or ballast keel bolt (if ballast external).

## RIGGING (MAST UNSTEPPED)

- ☐ Turnbuckles lubricated with anhydrous lanolin. Right-hand thread down. Equipped with toggles, Spares on board.
- ☐ All rigging pins lubricated. Cotter pins correct length, rounded.
- ☐ No longitudinal cracks in wire terminals.
- ☐ Mast straight. Track joints fair and aligned. Adjacent ends at each joint beveled on all sides to prevent "hang ups." Track greased with white Vaseline.
- ☐ All sail slides fair and rounded. (It should not be necessary to head into the wind in order to get the sail up if the corners of the slides are well-rounded to move freely in the track.)
- ☐ Hanks and shackles lubricated.
- ☐ Spreader attachment secure. Spreader tips checked for secure wire attachment under any tape and padding.

## Rod Stephens' Pre-Float Checklist: Sail

- ☐ Blocks and sheaves lubricated.
- ☐ Battens clearly marked. Spares carried for each one.
- ☐ Any sharp edges eliminated. (This holds true for everything on the boat.)
- ☐ If there are reel winches (not recommended), wire attached securely. No excess wire.
- ☐ On board; bosun's chair, bag of small lines, sail stops, sail covers, repair tape, waxed synthetic sail twine, good assortment of spare shackles and rigging pins.
- ☐ Sail bags clearly marked. (And sails should be clean and checked by launch time.)
- ☐ Mast wedges and (tight) mast coat at hand.
- ☐ Mast wiring and related electronic equipment tested.

**RIGGING (WITH MAST STEPPED)**

- ☐ Shroud rollers and turnbuckle boots installed.
- ☐ Windex and other masthead wind direction indicators aligned. Precise matching marks on aft centerline fixed part of wind guide, and marks for 0°, 30° left and right, 90° left and right, 180° on rotating skirt.
- ☐ Clear leads on all internal lines—mast and boom. Replacement gear on board.
- ☐ All standing rigging clean.
- ☐ Bitter end eyes for external halyards. Knots in ends of all the halyards.
- ☐ Limit bands painted on mast and boom (optional except for racing boats).
- ☐ Main halyard marked at top of winch drum to show position when top of headboard is at underside of black band (at 150-pound tension, equivalent to light-air sailing conditions).
- ☐ Jib halyards similarly marked (tension as above) at point beyond which further hoisting would damage halyard splices and/or mast sheave boxes.
- ☐ Cotter pins not spread more than 20°.

One of the most prestigious boat storage and maintenance operations in the Long Island Sound area is Norwalk Cove Marina, where hundreds of boats are berthed and serviced each year. Jack Haigh, long-time Norwalk Cove service manager, developed the check list that starts on the next page for power boats. It is based on many years experience dealing with problems after they'd developed, as well as in taking the steps that prevent their development. The checklist is not a one-time procedure; most of the items apply to almost every powerboat, and represent checks that should be made after any seasonal storage period.

**Jack Haigh's Pre-Float Checklist: Power**

# HULL/DECK/CABIN

**HULL**

- ☐ Scrape and paint bottom with a good grade of antifouling paint.
- ☐ Check all underwater gear (props, shafts, rudders, struts, cutlass bearings) for damage or wear, and recondition or replace as necessary.
- ☐ Check all through-hull fittings, including depth-finder transducers, for tightness before launching, and for leaks afterwards.
- ☐ Reinstall drain plug and tighten. Check for leaks when boat is launched.
- ☐ Wax, clean or paint topsides as necessary. Make sure paint is completely dry before the boat is lifted with a Travelift or crane to avoid marring.

**SUPERSTRUCTURE**

- ☐ Wash decks, and check all windows, hatches and fittings for leaks as you hose off the decks.
- ☐ Polish all metal hardware with an appropriate compound to protect it.
- ☐ Air out all canvas, check for mildew, wear or damage, and clean or repair as necessary. Lubricate all snap fittings to insure easy operation.
- ☐ Check and lubricate all on-deck and cockpit equipment (windlass, gin pole hardware, outrigger, fighting chair, davits, etc).

**FRESHWATER SYSTEM**

- ☐ Reconnect all pipes and hoses on pump and hot-water tank.
- ☐ Check wiring on pump.
- ☐ Fill water tank and check all fittings for leaks.
- ☐ Run system and check all faucets for proper operation and leaks.
- ☐ Check operation of hot-water heater.

**GALLEY**

- ☐ Clean and test stove for proper operation. On alcohol, kerosene and propane models, check for leaks and for proper fuel flow.
- ☐ Check refrigerator (and freezer, if installed) for proper cooling.

**HEADS**

- ☐ Open all intake and outlet valves, and check for ease of operation.
- ☐ Operate head, and check for proper intake and flushing.
- ☐ Check for leaks in system.

**ELECTRICAL SYSTEM**

- ☐ Check all panel switches and circuit breakers for proper operation.
- ☐ Check running lights, windshield wipers, blowers, instrument and compass lights, etc., for proper operation.
- ☐ Make sure spares for all bulbs and fuses are on board.

**ELECTRONICS**

- ☐ Remove electronics from storage and clean up.
- ☐ Reinstall equipment, making sure all contacts are clean.
- ☐ Check equipment for proper operation, and have it repaired or tuned as necessary by a qualified marine electronics technician.

# HULL/DECK/CABIN

## Jack Haigh's Pre-Float Checklist: Power

**STEERING**

☐ If cable steering, lubricate cable at helm and at rudder connections.
☐ If hydraulic steering, check for proper fluid level in reservoir and replenish as necessary. Check for leaks at helm unit(s) and reservoir.
☐ Check rudders for smooth operation.
☐ Check rudder ports for leaks, and tighten or replace as necessary.

**BILGE**

☐ Clean bilge while boat is on land, with drain plug still out.
☐ Check around bilge pumps for debris; remove any obstructions.
☐ Check for clogged discharge lines and leaking fittings.
☐ Check shower sump pumps in same manner as bilge pumps.

**ENGINE(S) BEFORE INITIAL START**

☐ Check oil level, and change or replenish as necessary.
☐ Check all belts and tighten or replace as necessary.
☐ Check water/anti-freeze level on freshwater cooled engine(s).
☐ Check lubricant level in transmission(s).
☐ Check condition of raw-water impeller, and change if it appears worn.
☐ Check clutch and throttle cables for full throw and ease of operation.
☐ Check all engine wiring for loose connections.
☐ Open fuel valves and check fuel filter(s) for dirt and/or water.
☐ Check engine alignment to propeller shaft (after boat is in water).
☐ Check shaft stuffing box for leaks, and tighten or repack as necessary.
☐ Check battery charge and electrolyte level; clean terminal posts.
☐ Tighten all battery cable connections at battery posts and at engine ground and starter terminals.

**ENGINE(S) AFTER STARTING**

☐ Check all water hoses and fittings for leaks; tighten or replace clamps.
☐ Check fuel lines and filters for leaks.
☐ Check ignition timing with timing light (gas engines).
☐ Check engine performance; change points and plugs if necessary.
☐ Check engine idle speed in and out of gear, and adjust if necessary.
☐ Check exhaust for leaks and proper water flow.
☐ Check all gauges for proper operation.

**SAFETY EQUIPMENT**

☐ Check all fire extinguishers and have them refilled and inspected as necessary. Have at least one extinguisher for every compartment.
☐ Inventory all Coast Guard required equipment, and check for proper operation.
☐ Inspect all personal flotation devices; replace any that are worn or torn.
☐ Inspect anchor and mooring lines; replace any that are worn or chafed.
☐ Check fenders; reinflate inflatable types if necessary.

## HULL/DECK/CABIN

**Winter Layup Time**

There are good reasons for giving the whole boat—hull and superstructure—a good scrubbing before it is covered:

1. There will be that much less dirt to scrub off in the spring.
2. Dirt tends to "eat into" and stain paint and gel coat surfaces. And sometimes the dirt penetration is so great after several months that the scrubbing required to remove it weakens the paint film or partially erodes the fiberglass gel coat.
3. Dirt and scum act as a kind of sponge that absorbs moisture, and thus serve as a breeding ground for mildew and wood rot spores.

Remember that the better your varnished brightwork is maintained, the longer the varnish will last. That's why it's always important to touch up bare spots as soon as they are noticed, rather than wait until the whole area needs recoating. This is even more important before winter storage.

Every bare or worn spot that you touch up now closes another avenue for water to enter the wood, and it definitely also adds to the life of the finish. Take an hour or two with a sheet of sandpaper, a small brush, and a can of varnish; cover all the bare spots you can find.

**Cleaning**

Cleaning the inside of the boat is even more important than cleaning the outside—if you don't want to come back to a really foul-smelling interior in the spring. Also, the bilges are much easier to clean with the boat out of the water because you can run a hose in there, use plenty of bilge cleaner, scrub where necessary, and then drain everything out by removing the plugs.

Don't leave standing fresh water on the inside where it can get into any woodwork. If leaving some fresh water is unavoidable, add rock salt.

Remove all leftover food and beverages, and clean the heads thoroughly—sinks, toilet, shower walls and floors. Temperatures under a winter cover can rise quite high on sunny days and fungus and mildew proliferate unless galley and head areas are spotlessly clean.

Ideally, all cushions, bedding, and curtains should be taken off the boat for storage ashore in a clean, dry spot; but if this is not practical at least make certain the cushions are in a dry spot on the boat, and use one of the various vinyl cleaner/polishers to clean them and give them a protective coating. Also, prop them up on edge so air can circulate around them as much as possible.

Spray curtains and similar items that must be left on board with an anti-mildew solution, and use this spray also on any lines left coiled inside any lockers. After everything has been cleaned, and all gear has been removed that will be stored elsewhere, prop all doors, hatch covers, and drawers open throughout the boat. This helps air to circulate and thus avoids the musty smell one often encounters in the spring.

Take a small can of lubricant and oil all the hinges, slides, catches and other moving parts of interior/exterior hardware. It may save the need for some replacement items next spring.

**Winter Covers**

Take your winter cover out of storage a week or so ahead of time so that you can inspect it for tears or mildewed areas that may need patching. If you are planning to buy a new canvas cover, then erect your supporting framework first so that you can measure it accurately for a better fit. Make certain the cover will have an adequate number of vents to allow for plenty of ventilation.

**Air Circulation**

When securing the canvas cover, it often helps to leave some openings at the bow and stern as an additional means of providing for ventilation on the inside.

Make sure the cover does not lay flat against the cabin sides or top, and try to avoid having it press flat against the transom or the topsides. One simple way to prevent this is to suspend a number of small fenders over the sides before securing the canvas—these will hold the canvas away and still permit tying it securely.

One big mistake many make is using light line that breaks easily when strong winds try to rip the canvas off. More damage is done to boats during the winter by canvas that flaps wildly around after a few pieces of line have broken than by the actual effects of the wind, snow and ice. So use a good strong line, and add more grommets to the cover if needed—most do not have nearly enough.

# GENERAL ACCESSORIES INVENTORY

List here gear and equipment not covered in other sections of this manual, items such as stereo sets, loud hailers, binoculars, flags, sails, and linens. This list will be of benefit to you when fitting out, or in establishing insurance claims in event of loss. Use brand names and model numbers.

| Quantity | Item | Date purchased | Location | Dates Serviced |
|---|---|---|---|---|
| | | | | |
| | | | | |
| | | | | |
| | | | | |

# TELEPHONE NUMBERS

Record here telephone numbers of mechanics, crew members, marinas, shoreside restaurants, yacht clubs

# PROPULSION

## Surveying Your Engine Installation

The boat with a Bristol-fashion engine arrangement is simply smoother, quieter and more reliable than one with careless work under the engine hatches. Consequently, if you are inspecting a boat with an eye to purchase, carefully consider the technical requirements of an engine room. As a matter of fact, why not carefully inspect the engine installation in your present boat, having repairs or alterations made (or doing them yourself) where you see that safety rules or good engineering principles are violated. What follows is a review of engine-room systems that deserve some well-informed scrutiny.

Above all, the inboard fuel system, gasoline or diesel oil, must be secure, tight, leak-free, and in accordance with the codes. Obviously, the consequences of problems here can be very serious. See that every inch of pipes, tubes, tanks and accessories is liquid- and vapor-tight. All parts associated with the fuel system must be well-supported and firmly installed. Watch for chafing of tubing; beware of long runs of unsupported fuel lines which might shake or vibrate loose. Such makeshift arrangements are taboo because of the danger of fire and explosions and must be repaired or reworked at once.

## Fuel System

Every component of the fuel system must be accessible to permit inspection or repair. Hunt for connections, filters, shut-off or transfer valves, traps or filters which are buried under the deck. Such clandestine arrangements are an invitation to trouble and should be reworked. In particular, manual shut-off valves should be located where they are readily accessible.

Fuel tanks must be tightly secured to the boat so that no magnitude of pitch, roll or pounding can loosen them. Vapor vents must be from the top of the tank. And you should see that all vents go outboard in such a way that expelled vapors cannot migrate back into the boat. Look carefully for the location where the fuel outlet pipe enters the tank. It *must* be at the tank's top, never at the side or bottom; should a leak occur there is the least chance of seepage with a top-mounted installation. Where you see any pipe, tube or valve enter the tank on its side or bottom, you are inspecting an installation which violates the safety code. All penetrations must be at the top of the tank; there must be no clean-out plates on the sides or ends of any tank.

The fuel-fill pipe should be secured to a deck plate and the pipe must be 1¼″ inside diameter or larger, as a smaller pipe tends to spit back fuel. There should be electrical continuity from the deck-fill plate all the way to the fuel tank, thence to the engine, to ground static electricity created when gas runs through the fuel nozzle or the nozzle contacts metal when being inserted or removed. Make sure that the fuel fill is located so that escaping vapors flow overboard, not into the cockpit or hull openings.

## Ventilation

Good ventilation is a definite safety requirement for the engine compartment; but ventilation must never be relied upon to remove flammable vapors from fuel-system leaks. The fuel system must be perfectly tight; *in addition,* ventilation must be good.

See that the engine compartment has a power blower. Determine that it exhausts overboard and that its air pickup is well below carburetor level in the engine compartment, because gas vapor migrates to the lowest area of the bilge. The lower the pickup, the better, so long as there is no danger of bilge water blocking it. Also make sure that the electric-blower motor is well above bilge-water level, so it doesn't get swamped when bilge water moves about. On most boats, this means that the blower should be a foot and a half above the lowest point in the bilge.

In addition to the blower system, adequate natural ventilation of the engine compartment not only promotes safety—as vapors are removed naturally when the blower is turned off—it also affords sufficient air for good combustion. Make sure that the engine compartment is fitted with cowls that permit the free flow of air into and out of the engine compartment. One or more forward-facing cowls or air scoops should be ducted to carry fresh air low into the bilge, below carburetor level. Similarly, one or more air outlets should be ducted to take stale air out of the bilge, and these outlets should also terminate low in the engine compartment where heavier-than-air vapors collect.

## Exhaust System

Simple but important, the engine exhaust system must be absolutely tight from engine to transom, so that no dangerous exhaust gas can find its way into the boat. Spent cooling water is spewed into the exhaust pipes of most installations and is depended upon to cool the system. Because they are water-cooled, many exhaust systems incorporate sections of rubber or neoprene steam hose. This is perfectly OK. But when you're inspecting a system, you must make sure that the hoses are clamped or, preferably, double clamped with stainless-steel hardware at all junctions with the pipe or tubing. See that the hoses are resilient and fresh, that there is no sign of corrosion or rust on the metallic sections. Run the engine, making sure that plenty of cooling water flows through the exhaust after the engine comes to temperature.

## Cooling System

Make absolutely sure that through-hull fittings for the cooling system are fitted with seacocks. If a hose breaks, quick action with a seacock valve will stop the leak. Check those vital seacocks for easy operation and accessibility. Hoses running from hull fittings to the engine must be in perfect condition, free of kinks and tight bends. Remember, a ruptured hose below the waterline can sink the boat. At low points in the engine cooling system you should find drain cocks or plugs which can be removed in the winter to prevent freeze-up. Where belts are used to drive water pumps, they should be easily accessible for inspection and replacement; the existing belts should be fresh and free from wear. There should be a zinc pencil or other device providing cathodic protection against corrosion in the engine's cooling system.

## Lubrication System

The best engine lubrication system incorporates an oil cooler serving the engine, with another serving the transmission. If the engine is a small auxiliary or of mild caliber, coolers may not be seen. But if it is a high-performance machine, it should have oil coolers. How about provision for easy oil changes? Some better engines, made by companies who love the boatkeeper, are fitted with built-in sump pumps which make oil changes easy. Snoop around and discover how easy it is to get at grease fittings and oil fittings on the accessories and controls.

The electrical system serving the engine and its immediate accessories should not have frayed or poorly secured wires, which are a sure indicator that the engine installation is an amateur job. In a good installation you will see wiring neat, trim, well-secured and with all connections made in a workmanlike manner. If the wiring is sloppy and not supported at frequent intervals, it invites a short circuit, which can lead to fire.

Starting batteries must be located close to the engine they serve. See that starter and grounding cables are as short and direct as possible, because unnecessarily long cables cause hard starting; they waste your battery's power. Battery clamps must be husky, clean and tight. Assure yourself that the battery or batteries are secure against possible movement in heavy seas. Furthermore, see that the batteries are in a well-ventilated location because, as they charge, flammable hydrogen gas is emitted. There should be clearance around and over the batteries so they can be easily inspected and serviced. In a good installation you will see battery boxes covered with a substantial, nonconductive, well-ventilated cover.

## Master Switch

A battery master switch—one having U.L. approval—is a desirable accessory. If the boat has two batteries, particularly if it is a twin-screw yacht, it should have a master-battery selector switch, marked 1-BOTH-2-OFF. This permits the operator to place either or both batteries on the line, or to disconnect both batteries entirely.

Confirm that there are no voltage taps on any battery. A 12-volt battery, for example, must not be tapped in the middle to furnish six volts for an accessory. If six volts is required, it should come from a separate six-volt battery having its own wiring. Two voltages floating around invite stray-current corrosion.

Test the throttle and clutch controls manually and visually. Both should operate smoothly, without binding or sticking. Each should have over-travel. In other words, the cable or linkage should be capable of more travel than required to completely open and close the throttle (or diesel fuel rack) and clutch lever. Unhappily, some new boats have controls which are inadequate and poorly adjusted.

## Alignment

The engine should sit firmly and squarely on its bed. Look for accessible adjustments on each engine mount or pad, and inspect the apparent workmanship on the engine stringers and bearers. If you care to delve more deeply, disconnect the prop-shaft flange from the engine's transmission flange. Slightly separate the two flanges. Their faces must remain absolutely parallel, and the shaft must not spring or deflect, nor need force in any direction when it is again coupled to the transmission. Here, you are checking shaft/engine alignment; if it is imperfect, the engine must be realigned in its bed.

## American Boat and Yacht Council

How good is that engine installation? If it comes through the relatively simple inspection delineated here, you can feel that it is technically acceptable, meeting the requirements of most codes. However, if you'd like to do a more thorough inspection, you may do so, guided by a copy of *Safety Standards for Small Craft,* the book of safety codes published by the American Boat and Yacht Council, Box 806, Amityville, N.Y. 11701. If you are interested in technical things related to boating, you should have this book.

—*Conrad Miller*

## Maintenance Information

Record here the specifications and maintenance information for engines, including those used with generators. The information should be contained in the owner's manuals supplied for the engines, and these manuals can be kept in the pocket inside the back cover of this book. By transferring the key information to these pages, you have a safeguard in case of loss of the manuals.

# PROPULSION

If you do not have a manual for an engine, it should be available from the manufacturer or a local dealer. For older engines where manuals may be out of print, you should be able to get specifications from shop manuals used by marine engine mechanics.

Note that the initial information is what you need to know for routine maintenance. Then more detailed specifications are noted for each system, plus necessary instructions in carrying out major maintenance operations.

Also in this section are general maintenance and trouble-shooting tips for both gasoline and diesel power plants, as well as layup and recommissioning instructions and some useful hints that will help you get the most efficiency from your engines. Information in Roman type applies to all types of motors. *Italic* type applies to gasoline motors only. **Bold** face text applies to Diesels only.

The sequence used for this section is that recommended by the American Boat & Yacht Council in its standard for engine manuals.

Where operating or maintenance instructions are called for, it may be easiest to photocopy the applicable information from the owner's manual and paste it in place in this section, either under the appropriate heading or on the blank pages provided. Include photographs (including those you take yourself) as well as sketches and diagrams.

If you have a separate generator motor, use the right hand part of the spaces to record appropriate information.

## Specifications Record

Warranty life,
conditions ______________________________

______________________________

Diesel fuel or
gasoline octane ______________________________

Outboard gas/oil
mix ______________________________

Filter/strainer
instructions ______________________________

______________________________

______________________________

______________________________

## PROPULSION

Lube oil type
& viscosity ______________________________

Oil change
frequency ______________________________

Crankcase capacity
w/filters ______________________________

Filter type ______________________________

Filter change
instructions ______________________________

______________________________

______________________________

*Oil operating*
*pressure* ______________________________

*Spark plug type* ______________________________

*Plug gap setting* ______________________________

*Plug tightening*
*torque* ______________________________

*Distributor point*
*gap setting* ______________________________

*Dwell setting* ______________________________

*Distributor*
*lubrication* ______________________________

______________________________

*Timing mark location* ______________________________

*Timing information* ______________________________

# PROPULSION

Electrical system voltage ______________________________

Polarity ______________________________

Intake valve clearance ______________________________

Exhaust valve clearance ______________________________

Cylinder head bolt tightening torque ______________________________

Compression pressure ______________________________

Transmission lube type ______________________________

Transmission lube capacity ______________________________

Trans. lube change frequency ______________________________

Trans. lube change instructions ______________________________

______________________________

______________________________

______________________________

Outdrive or reduction gear ratio ______________________________

# PROPULSION

**Fuel filter instructions** ______________________________

______________________________

**Timing mark location** ______________________________

**Timing instruction** ______________________________

______________________________

**Injector Nozzle identification** ______________________________

**Nozzle holder torque** ______________________________

Type & number of cylinders ______________________________

Rated hp/rpm ______________________________

torque/rpm ______________________________

Bore ______________________________

Stroke ______________________________

Piston displ. ______________________________

Compression ratio ______________________________

Maximum operating speed ______________________________

Firing order ______________________________

Weight ______________________________

# PROPULSION

## INSTALLATION

Exhaust pipe size ______

Intake water pipe size ______

Water scoop type ______

Fuel line size ______

Alignment instructions ______

______

______

## STARTING AND OPERATION

Normal weather ______

______

______

______

Cold weather ______

______

MAIN ENGINES GENERATOR

FUEL SYSTEM
GASOLINE

*Carburetor type identification* ______

# PROPULSION

MAIN ENGINES GENERATOR

*Carburetor adjustment instructions* ____________________

*Float chamber setting or fuel depth* ____________________

*Automatic choke setting* ____________________

*Sketch carburetor to show adjustment screw locations*

*Fuel pump type* ____________________

*Filter change instructions* ____________________

*Crankcase breather maintenance* ____________________

*Backfire trap maintenance* ____________________

## FUEL SYSTEM
## DIESEL

**Filter Instructions*** ______________________________

______________________________

______________________________

______________________________

**Lift pump operations*** ______________________________

______________________________

______________________________

______________________________

**Injector pump timing*** ______________________________

______________________________

______________________________

**Injector pump maintenance*** ______________________________

______________________________

______________________________

**Injector change procedure*** ______________________________

______________________________

*If necessary, make photocopies of information in owner's manual and paste in place here or on blank pages in this section. Include cutaway photos or diagrams where applicable.

# PROPULSION

## ELECTRICAL SYSTEMS & IGNITION

PROPULSION ENGINE(S) AUXILIARY GENERATOR

Battery Type ______________________________

Battery Amp/Hr ______________________________

*Coil Type* ______________________________

*Condenser Type* ______________________________

Recharging instructions* ______________________________

______________________________

______________________________

______________________________

Alternator (generator)
maintenance* ______________________________
Distributor
maintenance* ______________________________
Voltage regulator
type ______________________________

*Spark plug maintenance*
*requirements** ______________________________

______________________________

*Spark plug replacement*
*schedule* ______________________________

______________________________

*If necessary, make photocopies of information in owner's manual and paste in place here. Include cutaway photos, drawings, diagrams as applicable.

| COOLING SYSTEM | PROPULSION ENGINE(S) | AUXILIARY GENERATOR |
|---|---|---|

Drain plug locations ______________________________

______________________________

Anti-freeze capacity ______________________________

Anti-freeze type ______________________________

By-pass piping instructions* ______________________________

______________________________

Pump maintenance
requirements* ______________________________

______________________________

______________________________

Heat exchanger
closed circuit
capacity ______________________________

Heat exchanger
maintenance* ______________________________

______________________________

______________________________

Drive belt
adjustment* ______________________________

______________________________

Lube or gear oil
cooler information* ______________________________

______________________________

*If necessary, make photocopies of information in owner's manual and paste in place here or on blank pages in this section. Include photos, sketches, diagrams as applicable.

## PROPULSION

| COOLING SYSTEM | PROPULSION ENGINE | AUXILIARY GENERATOR |
|---|---|---|

Exhaust water outlet location ______________________________

______________________________

Exhaust water outlet size ______________________________

LUBRICATION SYSTEM

Filter type ______________________________

Filter change schedule ______________________________

Oil level instructions* ______________________________

______________________________

How to change oil* ______________________________

______________________________

______________________________

Lube requirements for special operating conditions ______________________________

______________________________

Special drive or accessory lubrication* ______________________________

______________________________

*If necessary, make photocopies of information in owner's manual and paste in place here or on blank pages in this section. Include photos, sketches and diagrams as applicable.

# PROPULSION

TRANSMISSIONS

Manufacturer ______________________________

Type ______________________________

Adjustment instructions* ______________________________

______________________________

Hydraulic fluid type ______________________________

Hydraulic fluid capacity ______________________________

Fluid Checking frequency ______________________________

Lubrication oil type & capacity ______________________________

Shift control instructions & warnings* ______________________________

Propeller shaft diameter & length ______________________________

Propeller type (blades & material) ______________________________

Pitch ______________ Diameter ______________

Propeller removal & installation instructions* ______________________________

______________________________

Shift control adjustments* ______________________________

______________________________

Instrument panel nomenclature* ______________________________

______________________________

*If necessary, make photocopies of information in owner's manual and paste in place here or on blank pages in this section. Include photos, sketches, and diagrams as applicable.

## PROPULSION

### When Your Gas Inboard Engine Won't Start

In a marine environment, the usual cause of an engine's failure to start is moisture—either wet wiring that shorts out the electrical system, or water in the fuel supply. Your first step in troubleshooting is to eliminate these possibilities, then to follow a logical sequence that will lead to the fault with little fuss, and no need for special equipment. You eliminate guesswork and unproductive random checks.

Begin by spraying all wiring with a moisture-displacing compound such as CRC or WD-40. Remove and clean spark plugs; wet, dirty porcelain on the exterior provides a low-resistance path to ground for the high tension voltage that otherwise would jump the spark gap. If the engine was spun a few times by the starter, plug tips should be damp with gasoline—an indication that the fuel system is okay; troubleshooting procedures under this heading should not be necessary.

However, if plug tips are wet with water, there's water in the fuel system. Drain and clean fuel filters; remove and drain the carbuetor float bowl; disconnect and drain fuel lines from fuel pump to carburetor, and from tank to fuel pump. If there's any reason to suspect water in the fuel tank, this should be drained and fresh fuel added. When working with the fuel system, be sure to observe all safety precautions: No smoking on the boat or in its vicinity; use of proper containers for drained fuel and proper disposal of these ashore, along with rags used to wipe up any spills. Ventilate and use the blower before trying again to start the engine.

Very few starting failures are caused by faults in the fuel system under normal circumstances, and the above procedures practically eliminate this system as a source of the trouble. However, if the engine still fails to kick over while it is being spun by the starter, make sure there's fuel in the tank (a gauge reading may be misleading, so try with a dipstick), and that the fuel shutoff valve at the tank is in the open position.

#### Battery and starter

Now check out the electrical system. Note that each step presents an "either/or" situation, so the steps are presented in outline form for the sake of clarity. Start by turning on the ignition switch.

### Battery

### Starter

I Ammeter needle doesn't move, or tell-tale "idiot" light doesn't glow: Battery is dead, or connection is broken between battery and ignition switch. Charge or replace battery as necessary; clean and tighten all connections; replace worn or frayed cables.

II Ammeter shows slight discharge, or tell-tale light glows: Current is flowing. Operate the starter.

A. Starter action is sluggish: Defective or partially discharged battery; loose, corroded or dirty battery terminals; mechanical failure in starter, defective starter switch or starter drive. Turn on a cabin light, supplied by starter battery voltage, that you can watch as you operate the starter again.

**What to Do When Your Gas Engine Won't Start**

1. Light goes dim, or out completely: Trouble is in the battery, or its connections or cables. Voltmeter readings should be 1.5 volts for each battery cell; hydrometer reading should show specific gravity of 1.250 or better. (See: Specific Gravity, page 69 under "Batteries."
   a. Low voltage or low specific gravity: Recharge or replace battery as necessary.
   b. Proper voltage and specific gravity: Clean and tighten battery connections and cable terminals. Replace any cable which appears worn or frayed.
2. Cabin light remains bright: Trouble is between battery and starter, or starter or its switch is defective.
   a. Make sure all cable connections are clean and tight.
   b. Have starter switch or starter itself repaired or replaced, as necessary.

**Ignition primary circuit**

**Primary Circuit**

B. Starter spins engine easily. Trouble is in ignition system. Make visual inspection to check for broken, worn, or disconnected wires. Remove distributor cap, block points open with a piece of cardboard, and use a voltmeter or test bulb to check for voltage at the terminal on the distributor.
   1. No current present: There's a break in the circuit leading back to the ignition switch, or the condenser has an internal short to ground. Disconnect condenser from the distributor plate so that its outside shell is not grounded; test again for voltage at the distributor terminal.
      a. Current is indicated. Condenser is faulty; replace it.
      b. No current shown: Check wiring connections at distributor; work back, checking for voltage at each connection, to the ignition switch. This will locate the faulty wiring or connection. Replace wiring or tighten connections as necessary.
   2. Voltage is present at distributor: Trouble within the distributor, most likely burned or dirty breaker points. Remove the piece of cardboard and rotate engine until points are closed. Check for current again at the distributor terminal.
      a. Current present: Points are defective; replace them. In an

emergency, points can be cleaned by using the sanded side of a match box, a knife blade, or the sharp edge of a screwdriver to scrape scale from the points. After cleaning, the points can be gapped to about .020″ by using four layers of newspaper as a feeler gauge.

b. Current not present: Causes include a weak or broken breaker arm spring, distorted or bent breaker arm, or nonconductive dirt on the points. Inspect and replace as necessary.

## Transistorized Systems

**Transistorized ignition systems**

If a capacitor discharge ignition system is used that incorporates the standard breaker points, the procedures outlined for testing a standard ignition primary circuit can be followed to some extent. If possible, disconnect the transistorized unit (or on some models, such as the Heath unit, simply switch to "standard") and re-wire to the standard mode. If the engine runs, the transistorized unit is at fault.

With other units, particularly breakerless systems, special equipment and procedures may be required. Check your manual.

## Secondary Circuit

**Ignition secondary circuit**

If the ignition primary circuit checks out okay and the engine still fails to start, test the secondary circuit. Remove the high tension lead from a spark plug and hold its end about ¼″ away from the block while the engine is being cranked by the starter.

I. No spark, or weak spark: Remove high tension lead from the center of the distributor cap (the lead from the coil) and hold it about ¼″ from the block while the engine is cranked by the starter.
   A. No spark, or weak spark: Faulty secondary coil winding; replace the coil.
   B. Good spark: Coil is okay; Distributor cap or rotor are faulty. Inspect and replace as necessary.

II. Good spark from spark plug lead: Ignition secondary circuit is good. Inspect spark plugs; clean and re-gap them, or replace as necessary. An emergency feeler gauge for the plug cap can be made by folding a piece of newspaper five times (this results in 32 layers of paper). When changing the gap be sure to bend only the side electrode and never the center one, as there is danger of breaking the porcelain.

**Spark Plug Note:** If you are used to looking at your spark plugs closely whenever you remove or change one, you should know what a normal plug looks like. If it's brown, light brown, grey—it's probably okay. If it's black and wet, it's saturated with fuel and oil. If it's loaded with carbon deposits it can be cleaned or replaced. (Since you always carry spares, you can replace when in doubt.) A plug that's been over-heating shows an eroded electrode, blistered insulator, or glazing of the insulator. These are symptoms—wrong type plug, engine over-heating, or other problems. Replacing will help temporarily, but you should correct the cause at the first opportunity.

**Spark Plugs**

Automotive books, such as "Basic Car Care," show you in color pictures what spark plugs look like under normal and abnormal conditions. Or get a mechanic to explain how he judges plugs by inspection.

### Fuel system

**Fuel System**

If for any reason you did not check for water in the fuel system, and there is no fault on the electrical side, the trouble must be in the gasoline feed. Remove the flame arrestor and make sure it is clean. Look down into the carburetor throat while operating the throttle linkage; the accelerating pump should push gas through the pump jet, which you can see.

I. Gas spurts from pump jet when linkage is operated: Choke action is probably defective. With a cold engine, the choke valve should be closed.
   A. Choke is closed. Engine is probably flooded with gasoline. Replace flame arrestor, open throttle all the way and crank engine with starter until it starts. (However, do not run starter more than 25 seconds at a time. Let it cool down.)
   B. Choke is open. Place the palm of your hand over carburetor throat as starter is operated; engine should start.

II. Gasoline does not spurt from pump jet: Fuel is not reaching the carburetor. Check fuel pump operation by disconnecting the line from it to the carburetor, and hold a container under the open end of the line. When the engine is cranked, fuel should pulsate out of the line. Be sure to take all safety precautions while working with the fuel system: no smoking on board or in the vicinity of the boat; wipe up spilled gasoline and dispose of rags properly ashore; dispose of any contaminated fuel properly ashore; ventilate and use blower before trying to start engine.
   A. Gas spurts from fuel pump: Carburetor float valve may be stuck, or float may be damaged so that its valve is jammed closed. Replace valve or float as necessary.
   B. No fuel spurts from pump: Make sure fuel shutoff valve at tank is in the open position. At the fuel pump, disconnect the line from

the tank, and if possible, blow back through it while someone listens at the tank (it may be necessary to disconnect each section of fuel line and blow through it individually to make sure it is not clogged.)

1. Bubbles are heard gurgling up into the tank as you blow through the line: Fuel line is clear; the trouble is in the fuel pump itself. Remove the sediment bowl and screen; clean and replace, making sure there's an air-tight fit. If the pump still does not function, it must be replaced.
2. Bubbles are not heard at the tank: Line is clogged. Remove each section of line and blow through it individually to clear it; replace any line that you can't clear by blowing through. Since a clogged line indicates foreign matter in the tank, it is best to have the tank drained or pumped out and fresh fuel taken on, after lines have been cleared or replaced. It's advisable also to add a heavy-duty filter and water separator unit at the tank end of the line to remove any substances not drained with the old fuel.

## Mechanical Failures

### Mechanical failures

The above procedures should locate the problem in almost all cases, particularly on an engine no more than a few years old. However, if the engine is getting a good spark at the plugs, and a fuel/air mix is reaching the cylinders, and it still fails to start, the problem must be a mechanical one. Most often this is a case of improper timing; the distributor housing has slipped on its shaft. Some engine manuals provide instructions for static timing, or a strobe timing light, if available, can be used while the engine is being cranked.

On an older engine, particularly one that has gone for a long period without an overhaul, burned and worn valves may cause lack of compression in the cylinders; a compression check will reveal ths.

If you don't have the information or equipment needed to check and adjust timing and compression, it's time to call in your marine mechanic.

# TELEPHONE NUMBERS

________________________________________

________________________________________

________________________________________

## Diesel Engine Trouble-Shooting

Because diesel engines do not have electric ignition systems or carburetors—the two most frequent sources of trouble in a gasoline marine engine—they not only require less maintenance than a typical gasoline engine, but are also more trouble-free in normal operation.

However, this does not mean that the owner of a diesel-powered boat never has engine trouble. Instead of a carburetor and ignition system, the diesel has sensitive injectors and a complex fuel-injection system that must not only be properly adjusted and timed, but must also be fed a steady flow of clean fuel that is not contaminated by the slightest amount of water or air in the lines. Air trapped in a diesel engine's fuel line, or water mixed in with the fuel, can result in all kinds of problems—a lack of power, misfiring of one or more cylinders, stalling, rough running, hard starting, or complete stopping of the engine.

Water is kept out of the fuel system by buying clean fuel from reliable sources when possible, by making certain deck filler pipes and caps are watertight, and by passing fuel through adequately sized multiple filters (which should be checked regularly) before it reaches the injection pump.

Air is kept out by making certain that all connections in the system, from the fuel tanks to each of the injectors, are good and tight. If a connection does work loose (these too should be checked regularly), then air bubbles will slip into the system and bleeding it to get rid of the air is the only solution. This involves opening a series of vent plugs located on top of each filter, as well as at various other points in the system, then manually pumping or forcing fuel through the lines until bubble-free fuel flows out of each opening (you open and then close one at a time, usually starting with the highest one on the engine).

Most diesel engines have built-in priming or pumping levers to facilitate this, and the owner's manual should give detailed instructions outlining the sequence to be followed. However, if you are in doubt about how this should be done, then you should contact the manufacturer or an authorized service depot for more details about the procedure. You can't always find an experienced diesel mechanic when you need one.

In addition to keeping air and water out of the fuel system, there is one other important point to remember: all diesel engines require large volumes of air while running. This means you have to make certain the engine room has adequately sized air scoops or vent openings for air intake into the engine room; and the air filters on the engine must be checked regularly to make certain they are not dirty or clogged, thereby restricting the amount of air that is actually reaching the cylinders. Your engine manual will tell you where these air filters are and how they can be cleaned or replaced when dirty.

By keeping these points in mind, and by consulting the troubleshooting information which appears on these pages, owners of diesel powerboats or diesel-powered auxiliaries should be able to track down the most likely sources of trouble when their engines fail to start or when they "act up" by not running smoothly.

Careful attention to procedural details plus patient checks of all potential trouble spots is probably the best investment any boatowner can make toward prolonging the life of his engine(s), and toward minimizing the likelihood of breakdowns.

Probably the single most important thing to do is to study the owner's manual before getting started. If you don't have the manual that came with your engine, order one from the manufacturer.

Although some manuals are sketchy in this department, the better ones will include illustrations that show you where all the drain plugs are for the cooling and lubrication systems, where the fuel and oil filters are located, how they are removed, and what kind of cartridges they need.

The manual will also include specifications giving the amount of coolant required, the number of quarts of oil the crankcase holds, the type of oil recommended, and other important data you should be familiar with.

## Winter Layup

Even if you prefer to let your boatyard or dealer do the winterizing, it is still important that *you* know what should be done, and how—and that you double check the list with your dealer to make certain everything has been attended to. Even the best of yards has mechanics who may get careless or forget something in the hectic rush of winterizing a large number of boats in a few short weeks.

## Checklist For Layup

Here is a checklist that applies to most inboard gasoline engines.

**___1.** Sometime before the boat is hauled, spend an hour or two in the engine compartment with a flashlight, screwdriver and a set of wrenches. Check all hose clamps to make sure they are tight, and replace any that are rusted, then spray one of the moisture-displacing lubricants on each to prevent corrosion and seizing-up. check mounting bolts and straps that hold cables and other controls in place, and be sure to lubricate wherever there are pivotal or sliding joints that must move freely.

**___2.** When the time comes for actual winterizing, run the engine until it's good and warm—better yet, take the boat out for a good ride—then shut the engine down and drain out all of the oil while it's still hot (on some engines you can remove a plug on the bottom of the pan; on others you have to pump it out through the dipstick tube). It's important you do this while the oil is still warm because sludge and metal particles will still be in suspension and will be drained out with the oil. Refill the crankcase with fresh oil, using the type specified for your engine.

___**3.** Replace oil filter cartridges with new ones.

___**4.** If the engine is fresh-water cooled and has a heat exchanger, check the amount of antifreeze in the coolant and add more if needed to protect the engine down to the coldest temperatures that can be expected, plus about a 20 percent safety margin. Remember that in most cases there should be at least 35 percent antifreeze mixed with the water to protect the engine against corrosion during the winter months, even if weather in your area doesn't get below the freezing point. Of course, if you do have freezing temperatures, it is best to do more than drain the block of fresh water. Some run the motor intermittently, after hauling, until heat dries out all water-jacket areas. Others use anti-freeze. See your engine manual.

___**5.** After adding antifreeze (if needed) run the engine until warm, then check coolant and oil levels. Top up as necessary.

___**6.** While the engine is running at a fast idle, remove the flame arrestor and slowly pour about one cupful of rust-preventive oil in through the carburetor to "fog" the insides of the cylinders with a light film of oil. If possible, stall the engine near the end by pouring the last couple of ounces into the carburetor rapidly.

___**7.** Clean the flame arrestor according to the recommendation in your owner's manual, then replace it on the carburetor.

___**8.** Shut off the fuel valve at the tank, then remove the fuel filters and clean out the sediment bowls. Then install fresh cartridges and replace the filters. Remember that on many inboard installations there are two filters—a large primary mounted on one of the bulkheads near the engine, and a secondary one on the engine itself (the primary filter is installed by the boat builder, so it probably won't be mentioned in your manual).

___**9.** If possible, drain all fuel out of the carburetor and out of the fuel lines leading to it, then remove each of the spark plugs and squirt a little rust-preventive or valve-top oil (about an ounce) into each cylinder.

___**10.** With the plugs still out, crank the engine over a few times with the starter motor, or by hand, to spread the oil around on the inside. Then replace the plugs.

___**11.** Remove all drain plugs and drain all the raw cooling water from the engine. Remember, if your engine has a fresh-water cooling system with heat exchanger, drain just the raw (salt) water, not the fresh-water coolant. As you remove each drain plug, check to see that water flows out easily—if not, clean the opening by probing through the hole with a piece of coat-hanger wire. Before replacing the plugs, dab a little grease over the threads to keep them from seizing up or rusting in place.

___**12.** Shut off the seacocks at the cooling water intakes, then disconnect the hoses just above them so the water will be drained out completely. Loosen the cover plate on the water pump to make sure all water is drained out of that housing also.

___**13.** Remove the batteries and arrange to store them at home, or have the yard store them. They should be in a place where they will be protected against freezing, and where a trickle charge can be applied.

___**14.** Loosen the tension on alternator and water pump drive belts, then spray all electrical connections with WD-40, LPS I or similar lubricant. Don't forget grounding cable connections, distributor caps and other places where moisture should be kept out. Squirt a little inside the distributor, the cam, and breaker points.

___**15.** After the boat has been hauled, bung the exhaust openings in the stern with oily rags, and disconnect the propeller shaft coupling where it joins the engine transmission to avoid undue stress on this connection when the boat is sitting on blocks. Wipe the shaft and coupling surfaces with oily rags to protect against corrosion.

Most authorities now agree that fuel tanks should be filled, with an additive fuel conditioner such as Stor 'n' Start included.

## Outboard Motors

___**1.** Outboards that are run normally in salt water should be flushed out with fresh water. Depending on the size and weight of the engine and on facilities available, this can be done by running it in a test tank or by using one of the various flushing attachments that permit hooking the water intake to a dockside hose.

___**2.** While the engine is still running at idle speed, remove the cowl and shut off the fuel valve. Immediately squirt some rust-preventive oil into the carburetor intake. Use the oil recommended by your motor manufacturer, and remember that the higher horsepower models have more than one carburetor. As the fuel in the carburetor(s) is about to be used up, squirt in an extra large dose of the oil to stall the motor.

___**3.** Take the motor out of the water and hold it vertical until all water drains out of the driveshaft housing. Then remove the drain plugs to let the rest of the water run out. Crank it once or twice by hand or with the electric starter to force water out of the water pump housing. Remember that the smallest amount of water trapped on the inside can freeze and crack a gear housing or water pump case.

___**4.** Drain the fuel tank, and all the fuel lines going from the tank to carburetor.

___**5.** Remove each spark plug, then squirt a few drops of preservative oil in through the openings and crank the engine over a couple of times to spread this oil around on the inside of each cylinder. Replace the spark plugs after checking them to see if they need cleaning or replacement.

___**6.** Use an oil can to lubricate all parts of the steering and tilt mechanisms, the throttle linkage, swivel pins, and all other parts that move or slide. Wipe unpainted metal surfaces with an oily rag, and touch up painted areas where the paint has cracked or peeled, or where signs of rust are showing through.

___**7.** Check lubricant level in the lowest part of the drive unit, following directions in your owner's manual, and add grease if necessary. Inject the grease through the filler hole at the bottom until it starts to flow out the air vent hole at the top. Then replace the plugs.

___**8.** Remove the propeller and inspect for nicks, dents or scratches, and send out for reconditioning if necessary. Clean the shaft with bronze wool, coat with a light film of grease, then replace the wheel.

___**9.** Remove the storage battery (if the motor has electric starting) and store it at home where it will be safe from freezing and where you can check its charge periodically—or let your dealer check it for you.

___**10.** If you are storing the motor at home, keep it where it will remain clean and dry; it doesn't have to be kept warm, however. A piece of canvas or cloth thrown over it will help keep out dust, but don't cover it tightly with plastic as this may lead to the formation of condensation inside the powerhead.

## Stern-Drive Engines

Since these engines are basically hybrids where a standard inboard engine is married to an outboard sterndrive not unlike that of a conventional outboard motor, most of the winterizing steps are already described under the lists given for Inboard Engines and Outboard Motors.

Start by following the first 14 steps for inboard engines, and then with the boat out of water and propped slightly bow-high (so that the engine is level or tilted slightly aft so that all water will drain out of the block), winterize the drive unit as follows:

___**1.** Lower the drive to the full-down position, but make sure it does not touch the ground. Remove drain and flushing plugs and allow all the water to run out. If the boat normally operates in salt water, flush with fresh water, following the directions in your owner's manual. When done, leave the petcocks open or the drain plugs out (place plugs in a plastic bag and tie firmly in place on the unit).

___**2.** Check oil level in the upper gear chamber or drive shaft housing, and add lubricant as needed. Then do the same with the lower gear housing. It is important that both these chambers be full of grease during layup to minimize the possibility of water damage.

___**3.** Lubricate steering linkage, using the grease or oil recommended by the manufacturer, including the gimbal housing pivot pins.

___**4.** Remove and inspect the propeller to see if repairs or replacement are necessary. Coat the shaft with grease and reinstall the propeller.

# PROPULSION

If your shaft has a zinc ring behind the propeller, check its condition; replace if necessary before the prop is reinstalled.

Modern marine diesels are generally simpler to winterize than gasoline models because they have no ignition system or carburetors. Also, diesel fuel does not tend to gum up the way gasoline does over a few months of storage, so there is no need to drain fuel lines.

Make sure you fill your tank completely before storing, as condensation is bound to cause bacterial growth when combined with any air present. Further, it may be useful to put a quart of fuel conditioner (MDR makes one called Stor 'n' Start) in the tank to insure against sludge formation.

## Diesel Engines

Diesels need attention to their cooling and lubrication systems, and these can be winterized by following the procedures outlined in steps 1 through 5 and 11 through 15 under Inboard Gasoline Engines. Religiously follow all instructions in your owner's manual.

*—Bernard Gladstone*

Paste in here photocopies of information, sketches, diagrams from owner's manual. Be sure to identify each item.

# PROPULSION

## Pointers On Commissioning

Most of the problems that develop with marine engines—in both powerboat and auxiliaries—are due to a lack of regular preventive maintenance, especially during and right after the layup period.

Like most mechanical pieces of equipment, an engine often takes more of a beating when it sits idle for months than it does when it is in constant daily or weekly use. Long periods of inactivity in a cold and often damp environment tend to encourage the formation of rust on unprotected metal surfaces, as well as condensation and pitting of electrical terminals and contact points; "seizing" of water pumps, valves and other infrequently moved parts; and loosening of bolts, nuts, hose clamps, and other fasteners due to alternate expansion and contraction of metal parts, or shrinking and drying out of hoses and flexible mounts.

That is why it is especially important that you take time out during the commissioning period to give your power plant and its associated mechanical and electrical components some much-needed attention.

Here are some of the important points that should be checked. Use the principles they imply on all your boat's running gear.

☐ Clean coil casing and high-tension lead, as well as contact points. Inspect all cables for fraying or deterioration.

☐ To insure full starting power, disconnect starter cables and clean terminal ends and bolts. Re-tighten securely.

☐ Clean and adjust points on distributor, or replace if needed. Then spray with moisture-displacing penetrating lubricant.

☐ Fuel filters should be changed at the beginning of each season, just to play safe. While doing this, replace gaskets and seals.

☐ Test engine mounts with wrench to see if they are right, and inspect rubber to see if it is badly deteriorated. If so, replace.

☐ Pay particular attention to fuel line connections. Test for "weeping" around unions with dry paper towel after engine is run.

☐ Run engine at fast idle until warm. Open heat exchanger cap and look for turbulence. Air bubbles could mean blown head gasket.

☐ Remove air cleaners and clean as recommended. Replace oil if yours is the oil-bath type. Make sure you tighten securely.

☐ Check stuffing boxes or packing glands to see if they need repacking. Some also hold grease that may need replenishing.

☐ Tighten every hose clamp you can find, especially those going to fuel tank. Replace clamps that are corroded or damaged.

☐ Don't forget mounting bolts around valve covers. Look for signs of oil seepage; it could mean you need a new gasket here.

☐ Check bolts with wrench to see if any are loose. Be careful about overtightening flange-mounting bolts to avoid distortion.

## PROPULSION

- ☐ Remove battery cables to clean terminals and cable ends thoroughly. After replacing, tighten firmly, then coat with Vaseline.
- ☐ Don't forget to inspect all parts of steering system; linkages, cables, chain, pulleys and mounts.
- ☐ To insure against water pump failure during the season, remove end plate to check impeller.
- ☐ Inspect all belts to alternators, pumps, etc. Replace any that show wear and adjust tension to each.
- ☐ See if the terminals on all cables—for clutch, throttle, etc.—work easily. Lubricate points on each.

Conrad Miller started sailing on Barnegat Bay at the age of six, and had his first book, *Small Boat Engines*, published when he was 19. About 40 years and one more book on marine engines later, he is on the engineering staff of Tenney Engineering Co., Union, N.J. and is a frequent contributor to *Motor Boating & Sailing*. He also is author of "Your Boat's Electrical System," published by Motor Boating & Sailing Books in 1973 and scheduled for re-issue in an updated version in early 1981. Miller is a member of the American Boat & Yacht Council and the Institute of Electrical and Electronic Engineers, and he has served as a consultant to the National Association of Boat & Engine Manufacturers Westlawn School of Yacht Design.

Bernard Gladstone has been home improvement editor of the *New York Times* for more than 20 years, and has been editor of the *Motor Boating & Sailing* "Boatkeeper" section since 1977. This section presents a wide variety of maintenance and improvement tips from the magazine's readers, as well as the major project features written by Gladstone. For six years he and his wife lived aboard their 48′ Egg Harbor before moving onto a 46′ Marine Trader trawler in 1978. He does all his own engine and general maintenance, and both boats featured interiors which he customized to meet his living and office needs.

# ELECTRICAL

## Wiring Diagrams And Color Coding

Trouble-shooting your boat's electrical system can be fairly simple if all wiring is color-coded according to the American Boat and Yacht Council standard (E-3)—and if you know the code. If you are rewiring an older boat, or adding electrical equipment to one now wired in accordance with the code, following the recommended practices will be a help to you, and others in the future, when it's necessary to track down a malfunction.

Under the standard, it should be possible to tell at a glance what circuit a given wire serves, particularly in the DC system fed by the boat's battery. Wiring for AC is color-coded to the extent that bonding wires, grounded current-carrying wires, and the underground (hot) wires can be identified as such. Bare wiring used as grounding and bonding conductors is not color-coded, of course. All other wiring on the boat must be insulated.

In AC circuits, white always is used for the grounded current-carrying conductors, with red and black used for the other two conductors in a three-wire system; and red, black and blue for the current-carrying conductors in a four-wire system. The grounded, white, current-carrying conductor in an AC system is considered the neutral conductor, and it is connected to the side of the AC source that is maintained at ground potential. It is *not* a bonding conductor. Where bonding conductors are part of the wiring, they are used to connect exposed metal enclosures of electrical equipment to ground in order to minimize shock hazard to the crew in case of a short in the equipment. These bonding conductors are always green.

Green is also used for insulated bonding wires in DC systems, and, as in AC circuits, this type of wiring does not normally carry current. Bonding wires in a DC system must not be confused with the negative (return) wires that run from the negative terminals of electrical equipment back to the common ground point for the electrical system. Unlike automotive practice, where the entire vehicle is used as "ground," and only a "hot" wire runs to each electrical component, a boat is wired with both positive and negative leads. All negative leads return to a common ground point, usually on the engine block. These negative leads may be either white or black, but, whichever color is used, it is to be maintained throughout the system to the exclusion of the other color.

Red is used in DC systems for the main leads from the battery to the starter, and thence to the starter/ignition switch, and to the ammeter. These lines generally are not fused. Fused circuits are those protected by fuses or circuit breakers.

## Color Coded Wiring

Beyond the ignition switch and ammeter, ten basic colors are specified for individual circuits, and some of these can serve more than one type of circuit. In these cases one use is associated with the engine, and the others have non-engine functions, which help to provide separation. Also, ABYC allows for addition of stripes to the basic colors as an aid in identification.

One of the basic colors does include a stripe to begin with: the yellow wire with red stripe that runs from the starter switch to the starter solenoid. This combination is used for no other purpose.

Yellow wiring is to be used between the generator or alternator field terminal and the field terminal on the voltage regulator. It is also the color for wiring from a fuse or switch to bilge blowers.

Dark gray wires should run from a tachometer sender to the gauge itself; this is also the color for navigation-light wiring, running between the fuse or switch to the lights.

Brown is used for the lead running from a generator armature to the ground terminal of a voltage regulator, and for wires from the generator or the alternator auxiliary terminal to a charge light—the little "idiot" light that goes on when insufficient current is being generated—and thence to the voltage regulator. Brown wires are also used for leads running from fuses or switches to bilge pumps.

Orange is the accessory-feed wire color for lines that run from the ammeter to a fuse or switch panel. It is also the color for the lead running from the ammeter to the generator or alternator output terminal.

Purple wiring should run from the ignition switch to the coil, and from the ignition switch to the distribution panel for electrical instruments, and from the panel to the instruments themselves.

Dark blue is the color for instrument and cabin lights, running from fuses or switches to the lights. Light-blue wiring should run from the engine's oil-pressure sender to the oil-pressure gauge. As in the case of all other instruments, there may be three wires attached: the purple "feed" line, the white or black negative-return line, and in this case a light-blue line that leads to the sensor.

Tan is used between the water-temperature sender and its gauge, and pink wiring runs from the fuel-gauge sender to the dial of its instrument.

If this color code is followed, the ABYC feels that a wiring diagram need not be supplied by the boat manufacturer. If some other means of identification is used, such as a different color code or numeral system, the proposed standard states that a wiring diagram should be provided that indicates the method of identification. In the case of another color code, the grounded return conductor must still be either white (preferred) or black (permitted).

It is possible, under the proposed standard, to use a single color for all wiring if colored sleeving or some other permanent means of applying color is used at all terminal points. Where numerals, letters, color coding or other identification is applied in the form of tape wrapped around a conductor, the tape should be at least 3⁄16″ wide and long enough to make at least two complete wraps around the wire. It should be visible near each terminal that the wire serves.

Where an electrical device has leads requiring polarized or selective connections, these leads should also be color coded in accordance with the proposed standard.

The ABYC standard calls for AC conductors to be loomed or jacketed separately from DC conductors when they must be run together in a common trough, tube or raceway.

While this is not yet an "adopted standard," it reflects the recommendation of experts in marine construction, engineering, insurance and related fields. By bringing your boat into line with this color code you can save yourself a lot of trouble and possible expense in the future.

Note that wiring size should be in accordance with ABYC Standards E-8 (AC Electrical Systems) and E-9 (DC Wiring Systems Under 50 Volts). In any rewiring work, or installation of new equipment, these standard should also be followed in regard to circuit protection, load distribution, and all other safety factors. See page 42 for information on ordering ABYC Standards.

## Batteries

Electrolyte nominal specific gravity varies slightly in different makes and designs of marine batteries. However, most manufacturers specify about 1.260 as the value for a fully charged cell. Specific gravity decreases as the battery discharges, increases as it charges. Consequently, its value is an approximate indicator of the battery's state. Between full charge and discharge state, a typical battery will evidence a gravity drop of 125 points: Full charge gravity is 1.260, half charge 1.197, and discharged 1.135.

Standard electrolyte temperature for hydrometer readings of specific gravity is 77°F, made when electrolyte level is above the plates. In order to

### Temperature Effect

get accurate gravity readings, the hydrometer float indication must be corrected for temperature and electrolyte level. The corrections are applied as follows:

1. Add one gravity point for each 3°F above 77°F; alternately, subtract one point of gravity for each 3°F below 77°F.

2. Subtract 15 points for each ½″ below normal level; alternately, add 15 points for each ½″ above normal.

From the above, it is apparent that a battery having electrolyte level ½″ above normal, and with temperature 107°F, will require plus 25 points correction. Thus, if the hydrometer reads 1.235, corrected value is 1.260, indicating the battery is fully charged.

### Altered Readings

Specific gravity is never tested immediately after water is added to the cells because the fresh water on top of the cells will make the reading much too low. Time must be allowed, and the battery used, to thoroughly mix the liquids. Battery manufacturers also say that age alters the normal gravity reading, pointing out that a decrease of several points a year is normal.

In order to split battery or AC power into fairly even loads for each branch circuit, you can compute to the total load for each circuit, and make adjustments as necessary.

In AC circuits, appliance and bulb loads are expressed in terms of *watts.* Watts are the product of voltage times current draw (amperes), and indicate power required for the time. Bulb sizes range from 40 watts to 100 watts for most lighting requirements (note that fluorescent lights give much more light than incandescent bulbs of the same wattages). Electronic gear and appliances may require anything from about 25 watts to 1,500 watts, with units that have heating elements (stoves, cabin heaters, hair dryers) at the high end. Wattages are stamped on bulbs, and on manufacturer appliance plates. Total the wattage on a circuit, divide by voltage (usually 115/120 volts AC), and you have the amperes drawn on the circuit with everything turned on.

In DC circuits, bulbs are marked according to current draw (amperes), and equipment may be marked in watts (particularly those with heating elements) or amperes, but total circuit load can be determined in terms of amperage.

In either case, if you determine that some circuits are carrying loads considerably heavier than others, it would be wise to re-wire in such a manner as to balance the loads. Of course heavy-duty appliances may require separate circuits for themselves.

# ELECTRICAL

### Ammeter Readings

An ammeter indicates *rate* of current flow *from* a battery (discharge) or *to* it (charge) while the engine is operating. If a battery is used for lighting direct current accessories, and it is not hooked into the charging circuit, an ammeter will indicate a current draw that depends on the number and wattage of lights or other units being operated.

If the ammeter in the engine charging circuit indicates a constant discharge while the engine is running, the generator or alternator may not be putting out enough current to compensate for the load on the entire system. An ammeter cannot indicate battery condition.

### Voltmeter Readings

A voltmeter indicates the potential power supplied to a circuit, the "electromotive force" (EMF) available from the battery. A battery cell of any type has a potential of a bit more than 1.5 volts when fully charged, no matter the battery size or type. Of course the larger the cell, the more *current* can be drawn from it over a longer period of time before the charge level becomes inadequate. Cells hooked together in series make up marine batteries of 6 volts, 12 volts, etc. Voltmeters can be used to check potential of individual cells as well as total battery voltage, and can give a quick indication of battery condition.

### Bonding

Bonding a boat's direct current electrical system provides a low-resistance path to ground between otherwise isolated metal objects within a boat, particularly those in contact with sea water. This helps prevent possible existence of a voltage potential on exposed metal enclosures of electrical equipment, provides a path to ground for possible lightning strikes, and helps to reduce radio interference on a boat. The bonding system should be in accordance with American Boat & Yacht Council safety standard E-1 (See page 42 for information on ordering ABYC standards).

### Choosing Right Generator

One thing that often confuses the boatowner who decides to install a generator is estimating the capacity needed. To do this you must have an estimate of the electrical load likely to be encountered, so you can select a generator whose output (in kilowatts) will be equal to that load.

The table that follows gives typical wattages for many of the electrical appliances that are likely to be used on board, so you can easily add up the total wattage needed (remember that one kilowatt is equal to 1,000 watts):

|  |  |
|---|---|
| Air conditioners | 500 to 1,500 watts (depending on size) |
| Battery Chargers | 400 to 900 watts |
| Clothes Dryer | 1,500 to 4,000 watts |
| Coffee Maker | 600 to 800 watts |

## ELECTRICAL

|  |  |
|---|---|
| Electric Drill | 250 to 500 watts |
| Dishwasher | 1,200 to 1,500 watts |
| Electric Range | 550 to 1,500 watts per element |
| Frying Pan | 1,000 to 1,350 watts |
| Hair Dryer | 550 to 1,000 watts |
| Heater | 1,000 to 1,300 watts |
| Refrigerator | 350 to 450 watts |
| Television, color | 250 to 300 watts |
| Washing Machine | 400 to 550 watts |
| Water Heater | 1,000 to 1,500 watts |

### Circuit Loads

When adding up these figures, remember it is highly improbable that all your lights and appliances will be on at the same time. This means you do not need a generator capable of handling the total potential draw of all appliances simultaneously. The sensible way to compute the size of the generator you will need is to figure on the largest *probable* load you are likely to encounter *at any one time.*

Then try to pick a generator that is capable of delivering at least this much plus a small safety margin. However, don't forget that electric motors and motor-driven appliances require considerably more power when starting—anywhere from two to four times as much power is required during the intitial surge. (The figures listed in the table above are the typical loads when running.)

### Winterizing

Electronic gear such as depthfinders, radios, RDFs, and similar items that unplug easily for removal should be taken off and stored at home in a dry location. This is as much to prevent theft during the off-season as it is to protect the equipment against exposure to cold and dampness. Clean the outside of each case carefully, then wrap in plastic to keep dust out.

Larger pieces of gear that do not unplug easily—such as radar units or autopilots—are best left in place, but it is a good idea to wrap each with a piece of clean canvas to keep the dust out. (Wrapping these items in cloth is better than plastic because fabric is less likely to cause condensation on the inside.)

The rest of the boat's electrical components—terminal blocks, fuse panels, circuit breaker panels, switches—should be visually examined and all terminal nuts and screws checked for signs of looseness or excessive corrosion (replace those that are badly corroded). Tighten any connections that are loose, and clean those that look dirty. Then spray all of them with one of the moisture-displacing penetrating lubricants such as WD-40, LPS1, CRC or a similar product.

# ELECTRICAL

## Batteries

One important electrical item that should not be neglected is the storage battery (or batteries). If it is to be left on board during the winter because the boat will remain in the water, and you want the battery as a source of power for your bilge pump, then make sure it is kept fully charged at all times. Your boat's automatic charger will handle this easily, if you have one on board, or you can arrange to come down and plug in a trickle charger periodically as needed. (Note: If you store your boat in the water, make sure you have carefully read your insurance policy. Some policies are specific on this point, others are vague. In one case we know of, the boat was "decommissioned" in the water but the battery was left aboard. Damage occurred, a claim was made, and the insurance company refused to pay, stating that because the battery was still aboard the boat was still in commission, and not covered under the storage policy. If your policy is vague, get written clarification.)

For boats that will be hauled and stored on land, the best way to take care of the battery is to remove it and store it in a dry location (it does not have to be heated) where it can be kept charged with periodic use of a trickle charger. The battery should have its posts cleaned and checked for looseness, then the top rinsed off with a mild solution of ammonia and water. Check the water level in each cell, and make sure the battery is fully charged (check this with a hydrometer) before storing.

To protect running lights and other exterior lights from corrosion and from having bulbs "frozen" into place by oxidation, remove the lenses and spray the bulb sockets and insides with LPS1, WD-40 or similar protective spray. Smear a light film of Vaseline over the lens gasket and the rim of the lens before replacing it, but install a new gasket if the old one looks cracked or dried out.

In the chapters on tools and propulsion you will find useful information on tools and spares for electrical work, on sprays that waterproof ignition systems, and on certain kinds of electrical trouble-shooting. Much of this information applies to the non-propulsion electrical components of a boat, including electronic equipment and lighting. A useful book in this field is "Your Boat's Electrical System, 1981-82" by Conrad Miller and E. S. Maloney.

*—Tom Bottomley*

WIRING DIAGRAMS and COLOR CODING

Draw wiring diagrams in the space on next page, or make photocopies of diagrams supplied by the boat and equipment manufacturers, and paste them here. Use felt-tip pens with translucent inks to color each circuit line to match the actual wiring. Where wiring has two or more colors, use all the colors on the diagram either paralleling the line or in alternating dashes along it. Colors often are given as abbreviations on wiring diagrams, but by adding the actual colors, you make it much easier to trace each circuit. If changes are made, mark it on the diagram!

**CIRCUITS ADDED OR ALTERED:** Give date and describe work done. If possible, draw diagram that shows circuit as it now exists, using color codes as previously described.

## Circuits Added, Circuits Altered

______________________________

______________________________

______________________________

______________________________

______________________________

## Bulb List

NAVIGATION LIGHTS

| TYPE | VOLTS | AMPS | SPARE |
|---|---|---|---|

BOW ______________________________

SIDE LIGHTS ______________________________

AFTER RANGE ______________________________

STERN ______________________________

MASTHEAD (SAIL) ______________________________

SPREADER ______________________________

## Cabin Fixtures

CABIN FIXTURES______________________________

______________________________

OTHER ______________________________

______________________________

# RIGGING/HARDWARE

## ROD STEPHENS

## On Going Aloft

Going aloft used to be easier. Much of my early experience was on boats with ultra-conservative aspect ratios and gaff rigs with sturdy mast hoops to hold the luff of the mainsail to the mast. The hoops provided a convenient and safe stepladder arrangement right up to the gaff. Quite often, by standing on the gaff or on the spreaders that were just a little higher, you could reach whatever had to be dealt with. Even when there was some motion, the low aspect ratio minimized the effort of the boat to shake you off.

With the swing to the Bermuda rig, aspect ratios increased, but rather gradually. Many of the boats were quite narrow and sailed well up to 35° or 40° heel angle. If you could match a good breeze and smooth water with a helmsman you could trust, it wasn't hard to "walk" up the mast, especially when there was a good handful of external halyards as an assist, and as long as the really wide heel angle was maintained and the spar was dry enough to provide good footing. Still, if there was more to do than impress the passengers, it was better to use the bosun's chair.

The swing to wider boats that have the sail more upright and the general cleaning up of the rig, which includes leading most halyards inside the spar, has forced us to rely more on the bosun's chair. At the same time, the job of those on deck has changed from just taking up slack to straightforward hoisting. Given these facts, what is the best kind of chair?

The best type—particularly if you want to get something out of your pocket (difficult with a canvas sling type)—has a plywood bottom crisscrossed underneath by synthetic lifting ropes that form a back-up (see drawing next page).

The hoisting apex of this bosun's chair should have a 5⁄16″ by 2″ outside diameter ring or 5⁄16″ bow shackle, with the lines seized tightly around. The length of the line should be kept to a minimum so that the hoisting point is as close as possible to the chair bottom. This is important for two reasons: First, it enables you to hoist the chair higher up, simplifying the difficult-to-reach jobs at the top of the mast. Second, the person in the chair is more

# Rod Stephens On Going Aloft

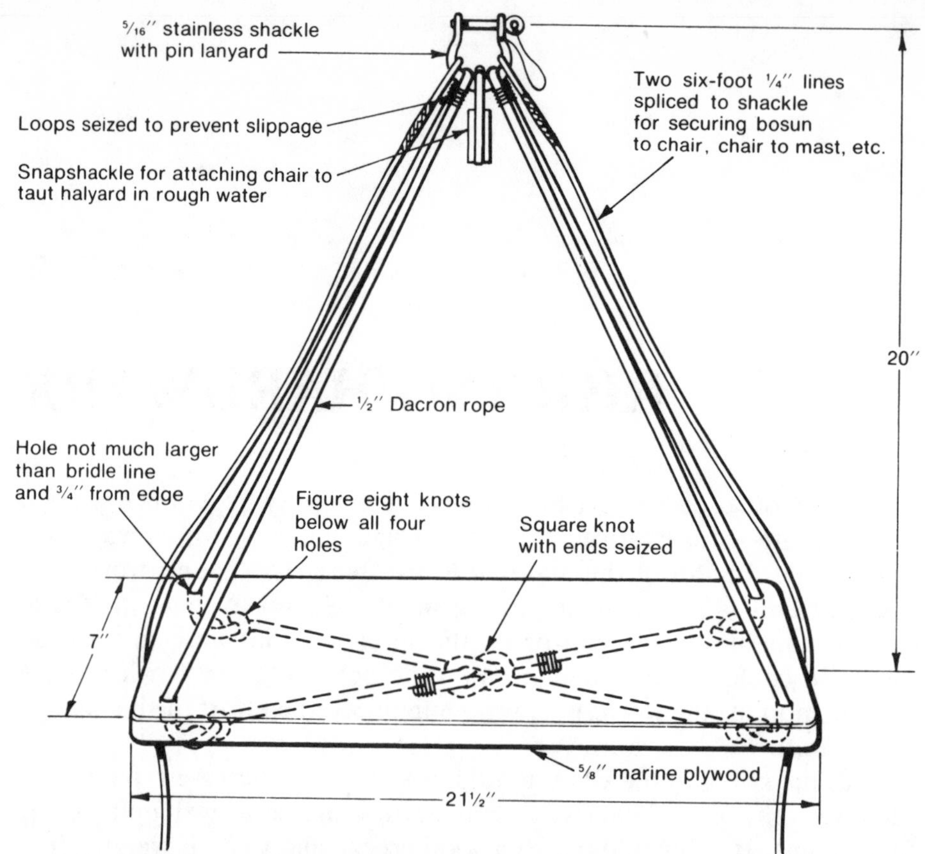


*Rod Stephens prefers this type of bosun's chair. He points out that the board can be painted or varnished except for the center area that is the actual seat—leave this bare wood. Distance between the corner holes is 5½″ on the short side and 20″ on the long side.*

secure, because it is difficult to slide out in either direction.

The chair lifting lines go through reasonably tight holes on each corner of the chair bottom, and there should be figure eight knots in the bridle, immediately below each of the corner holes. These knots prevent the chair bottom from sliding or tipping, which makes going aloft safer and permits the masthead man to devote more of his energy to the job in hand and less to self-preservation.

The lines should be about ½″ diameter and—most important—should be synthetic. I remember one spring day in City Island, New York, when I was swinging around aloft on what looked to be a pretty good chair with manila bridle lines. After one rather extreme swing out around the forestay to get to the other side, I happened to notice that one strand of the three-strand rope had carried away. I immediately put an extra line under my shoulders and hitched around the halyard, and asked to be lowered as smoothly as possible. When I reached the deck, it was quite easy to break

## Rod Stephens On Going Aloft

the line—or what was left of it. Moral: shoulder the extra cost and use synthetic.

You should fit your chair with two ¼″ diameter lines, each about six feet long and spliced under the shackle or ring. Their primary function is to secure you in the chair when necessary, and to secure the chair in the position desired when working aloft. It is also a good idea to hitch on a couple of similar lines that can be disconnected when needed. These can secure something you may be working on which has to be temporarily unfastened during the operation.

In rough weather, an extra halyard—if available—should be set very tight against the mast. A snatch block snapped around this halyard and hooked into the hoisting part of the chair should provide added security against the possibility of swinging away from the mast and colliding with it. A rough landing can result in injury to the occupant of the chair.

In addition to these short lines, there should be in really rough weather two strong tag lines, one leading from each side of the chair bottom. They can be secured to the crisscrossed lines under the chair with bowlines and should lead to strategic deck positions and be carefully tended throughout the hoisting operation to maintain tension so that the gyrations of the chair are minimized. When lowering, these tag lines should be taken in steadily for the same purpose.

No one should go aloft when it is rough without being strongly secured to the chair. If there is a bad collision, at least the injured person can be lowered without falling in the water.

In addition, it is a good fundamental rule to wear long pants and long-sleeved shirts, and to double up everything to provide padding when conditions are rough. It's also essential to eliminate sharp objects aloft while fitting out. Either pad them or round them.

## Working Aloft

There are chairs with various pockets for tools and gear. This is well and good, but in case you don't have such a fine arrangement, be sure to have a deep canvas bucket with rings at top and bottom. A bag type of bucket is no use as you cannot see what's in it, and it's hard to come up with what you want when you reach in and the bag closes around your hand.

Any tool of real weight should be securely tied with a light line to the lifting ring in the chair. The lines should be long enough to permit using the tool without disconnecting it. It's all too easy to lose your grip on a wrench or large screwdriver when you are putting a load on it. It may get to the deck before anyone has time to dodge it. Even if it doesn't hit someone, it may damage the deck. Beyond that, I've yet to see a good wrench or screwdriver that knows how to swim.

# RIGGING/HARDWARE

## Rod Stephens On Going Aloft

Generally, it's better to avoid any kind of snapshackle. If you must use one, tape it for good luck and, as a precaution, take one of the small lines and hitch it securely around the halyard just above the snapshackle.

When there's a choice, it's good to go up the weather side abaft the mast, presuming the mainsail is set so the luff of the mainsail will minimize the amount of swinging, at least in one direction. Also, depending on the importance of the job and the state of the sea, remember that bringing all the sea abeam while keeping enough sail to minimize rolling gives you the best chance to go aloft and do the job safely.

Before going up, it's a basic rule to test the chair by securing it to the halyard and jumping up and down as hard as you can. It's better to spot a potential weakness (looseness, a crooked line-up) at 18″ above the deck than when you're at the top of the mast.

An all-rope halyard lets the person going aloft help a lot by going hand-over-hand on the hauling part. If the halyards are all internal and if there is a shortage of power on deck, you can use an internal halyard to hoist up a single block with an all-rope external halyard temporarily rigged.

## Hoisting

Those hoisting on deck should avoid excessive winch turns that are all too frequently used in a misdirected quest for additional security. Four turns is the absolute maximum. Remember that excessive turns considerably waste power and increase the chance of fouling.

Self-tailing should be used only when there is no alternative, and only if the line easily matches the self-tailing gear and arrangements are such that the line coming off leads down in such a manner that its weight puts some tension on the line feeding off to help the effectiveness of the self-tailing gear.

Never use reel winches when going aloft.

Remember to go slowly both up and down when passing spreaders or any other obstructions such as a radar antenna and any fore and aft stays. Hand motions are very effective to signal those below. Some simple ones are clenching a fist for "stop" or "hold," moving the hand in a circular motion for "go ahead," and pointing up and down to indicate direction.

When it is rough, the person aloft should be particularly careful to avoid putting unreasonable fore and aft loading on spreader ends. This is especially important for a large person on a relatively small boat.

When the foretriangle is less than masthead, there should be an arrangement that makes it possible from the deck to rig a gantline (temporary halyard) that can be pulled through at the masthead, presumably using a messenger that might also serve as a flag halyard. This can be important in case there is a problem with a main halyard.

In case of heavy work to be done, two chairs can be useful. I can

## Rod Stephens on Lowering

remember three or four aloft on one Twelve Meter on the way to the starting line when a lot of last-minute work was needed the day after a dismasting.

As for coming down, again avoid extra turns. Two full turns generally suffice, but this depends a little on the relative weights of the person being lowered and the person tending the halyard. The target is to pay out line smoothly all the way, and to avoid the usual stop and go that is uncomfortable and creates unneccessary peak loads.

Just one more tip: When the option exists, always come down directly over the person tending the halyard. This invariably improves his concentration!

—*Rod Stephens*

## Hardware and Rigging Checks

The following check list on deck fitting and machinery, and standing and running rigging, has several uses. That's why there are three boxes after each item.

One box can be used to check that each item is aboard when a new boat is delivered, or when a boat is outfitted at the beginning of the season.

Another box can be used to check before an important cruise or race.

The third box can be used for lay-up time—items to be taken home, turned over to a rigger for checking, or repaired.

**Deck Fittings and Machinery**

| Fittings & Fastenings: | | Machinery: | |
|---|---|---|---|
| Chocks | ☐☐☐ | Windlass—General | ☐☐☐ |
| Bitts | ☐☐☐ | Drum | ☐☐☐ |
| Cleats | ☐☐☐ | Wildcat | ☐☐☐ |
| Ring Bolts | ☐☐☐ | Wildcat Lock | ☐☐☐ |
| Pad Eyes | ☐☐☐ | Pawls | ☐☐☐ |
| Fairleads | ☐☐☐ | Pawl Ring | ☐☐☐ |
| Sheet Travelers | ☐☐☐ | Brake | ☐☐☐ |
| .................... | ☐☐☐ | Bar | ☐☐☐ |
| Rail Stanchions | ☐☐☐ | Fastenings | ☐☐☐ |
| Rails or Man Ropes | ☐☐☐ | Winches—General | ☐☐☐ |
| Rail Turnbuckles | ☐☐☐ | Pawls & Rings | ☐☐☐ |
| Fastenings | ☐☐☐ | Fastenings | ☐☐☐ |
| Davits | ☐☐☐ | Handle | ☐☐☐ |
| Sockets | ☐☐☐ | .................... | ☐☐☐ |
| Brackets | ☐☐☐ | .................... | ☐☐☐ |
| Falls | ☐☐☐ | .................... | ☐☐☐ |
| Fastenings | ☐☐☐ | .................... | ☐☐☐ |

# RIGGING/HARDWARE

**Running Rigging**

**Running Rigging**

| Halyards | Line | Splices | Thimbles | Blocks | Shackles |
|---|---|---|---|---|---|
| .................. | □ □ □ | □ □ □ | □ □ □ | □ □ □ | □ □ □ |
| .................. | □ □ □ | □ □ □ | □ □ □ | □ □ □ | □ □ □ |
| .................. | □ □ □ | □ □ □ | □ □ □ | □ □ □ | □ □ □ |
| .................. | □ □ □ | □ □ □ | □ □ □ | □ □ □ | □ □ □ |
| Sheets: | | | | | |
| .................. | □ □ □ | □ □ □ | □ □ □ | □ □ □ | □ □ □ |
| .................. | □ □ □ | □ □ □ | □ □ □ | □ □ □ | □ □ □ |
| .................. | □ □ □ | □ □ □ | □ □ □ | □ □ □ | □ □ □ |
| .................. | □ □ □ | □ □ □ | □ □ □ | □ □ □ | □ □ □ |
| Running Backstays ... | □ □ □ | □ □ □ | □ □ □ | □ □ □ | □ □ □ |
| Topping Lifts ........ | □ □ □ | □ □ □ | □ □ □ | □ □ □ | □ □ □ |
| Outhauls & Downhauls .......... | □ □ □ | □ □ □ | □ □ □ | □ □ □ | □ □ □ |
| Lazy Jacks .......... | □ □ □ | □ □ □ | □ □ □ | □ □ □ | □ □ □ |
| Gantlines ........... | □ □ □ | □ □ □ | □ □ □ | □ □ □ | □ □ □ |
| .................. | □ □ □ | □ □ □ | □ □ □ | □ □ □ | □ □ □ |

**Spars and Standing Rigging**

**Spars and Standing Rigging**

| | | | |
|---|---|---|---|
| Mainmast—General...... | □□□ | ..........Mast—General | □□□ |
| Boom ................ | □□□ | Boom ............... | □□□ |
| Spinnaker Boom....... | □□□ | Struts or Spreaders..... | □□□ |
| Whisker Pole.......... | □□□ | Shrouds & Stays ....... | □□□ |
| Struts or Spreaders..... | □□□ | Backstays............. | □□□ |
| Shrouds & Stays ....... | □□□ | Chain Plates .......... | □□□ |
| Backstays............. | □□□ | Turnbuckles .......... | □□□ |
| Chain Plates .......... | □□□ | Masthead Sheaves ..... | □□□ |
| Turnbuckles .......... | □□□ | Cheek Blocks ......... | □□□ |
| Masthead Sheaves ..... | □□□ | Sail Track ............ | □□□ |
| Cheek Blocks ......... | □□□ | Spare Turnbuckles ..... | □□□ |
| Sail Track ............ | □□□ | ...................... | □□□ |
| Lightning Arrester ..... | □□□ | ...................... | □□□ |
| ...................... | □□□ | ...................... | □□□ |

Note: good sources of information on rigging and hardware, with illustrations and specifications, are catalogs such as those available from suppliers such as Wilcox-Crittenden, Middletown, CT 06457, Merriman-Holbrook, 301 River St., Grand River, OH 44045, and Nicro/Fico, 2065 West Avenue 140th, San Leandro, CA 94577.

## Tom Parrett on Tuning Your Rig

Some cruising people tend to think that a well-tuned rig is strictly for racing boats. This can be a dangerous misconception. A poorly tuned rig, besides making your boat sluggish, may also put unnecessary strains on the mast, shrouds, stays, and hull, and perhaps shorten the life of your sails.

Masts, whether wood or extruded aluminum, are very strong in compression when they are held straight, but when they are allowed to bend, the compression exerts forces the mast was not designed to sustain. In general, then, a well-tuned mast is perfectly vertical, and held firmly in place by standing rigging of an adequate size.

Initial tuning begins with the bare rig at the dock. First, position the mast vertically fore and aft (unless, of course, rake is desired for proper balance; your spar and rigging plan should show the amount of rake). Determine whether the boat is in trim or not. Eye the boat broadside from shore or another boat. Then sight up the mast from deck level as if you were aiming a gun: Press your check against the mast and close your outward eye. Sight up all four faces of the mast—starboard, port, forward, aft—at first, just to see what you're dealing with. Then restrict your sightings to whichever two faces you are tuning.

Also, the main and genoa halyards can be effectively used as plumb lines. Free the business ends of both halyards and drop the genoa halyard to a few inches above the deck, the main halyard to a few inches above the gooseneck. (Be sure to cleat the bitter end of the halyard!) They will both hang close to the mast amid-ships when the mast is straight. Tighten one stay and loosen the other to achieve this position.

If your mast steps on the keel, remove the partner wedges and center the mast in the deck opening, giving the mast a nudge now and then during adjustments to settle it in position. (Be sure the mast hole itself is centered—builders' tolerances may allow some leeway here. Check by measuring from the side of the hole to each rail.) The mast must be in column from butt through the partner all the way to the truck.

When the mast is vertical fore and aft to your satisfaction (sight up the mast again), tighten the headstay and backstay equally using hand tension on the turnbuckles. For leverage, employ an average-sized screwdriver inserted through the center of the turnbuckle. The stays should be taut but by no means straining. Pull with your weight against the stays—the average yachtsman should find them deflecting about two inches.

(There is, of course, a more exact measurement for proper initial tensioning. If you have a tension gauge—Loos sells an inexpensive one—tighten all standing rigging to 20 percent of its breaking strength. The builder should be able to tell you the rigging's breaking strength; if not, any rigger or wire rope manufacturer can.)

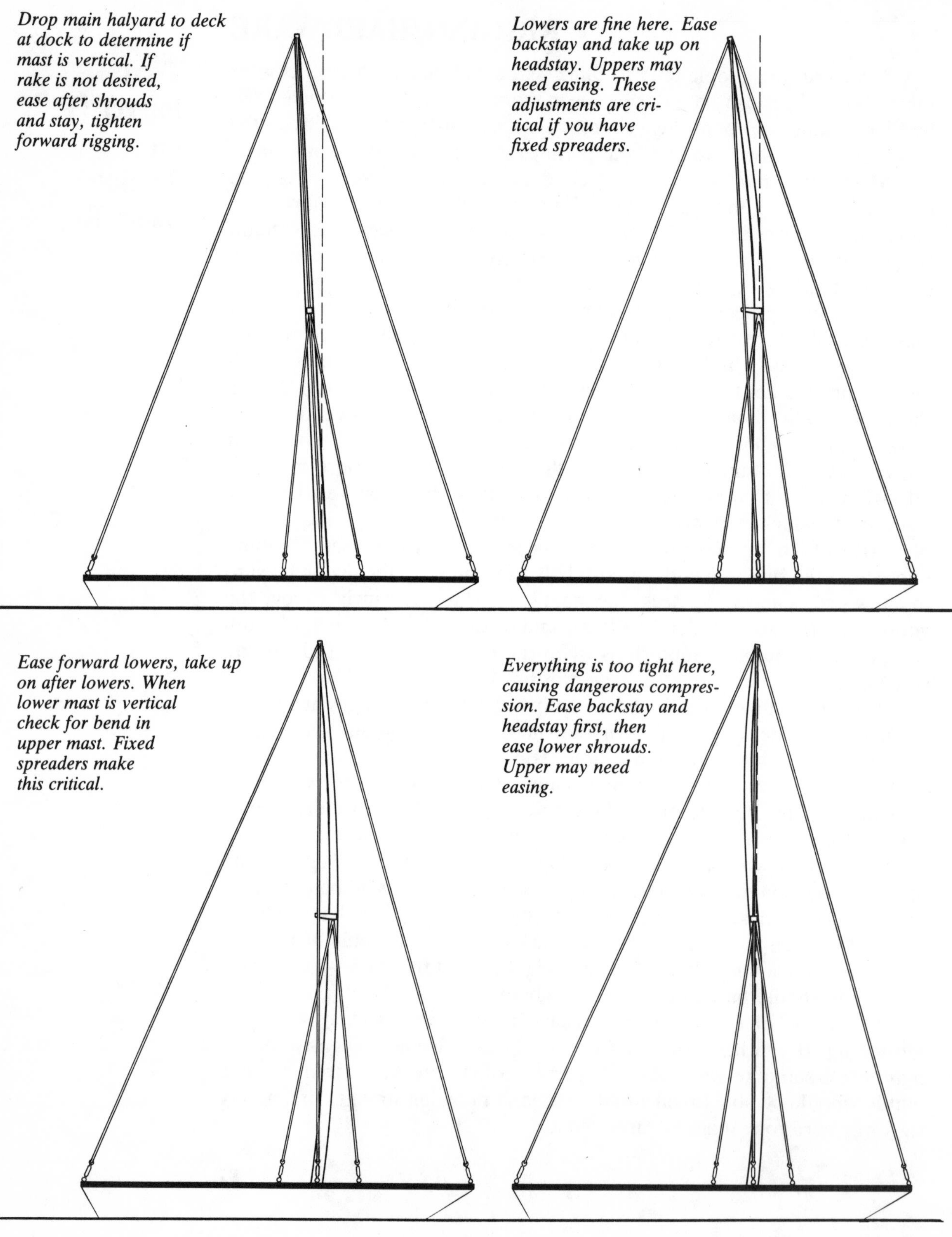
*Drop main halyard to deck at dock to determine if mast is vertical. If rake is not desired, ease after shrouds and stay, tighten forward rigging.*
*Lowers are fine here. Ease backstay and take up on headstay. Uppers may need easing. These adjustments are critical if you have fixed spreaders.*
*Ease forward lowers, take up on after lowers. When lower mast is vertical check for bend in upper mast. Fixed spreaders make this critical.*
*Everything is too tight here, causing dangerous compression. Ease backstay and headstay first, then ease lower shrouds. Upper may need easing.*

Next, center the mast amidships. Run a check by dropping a masthead halyard to just above deck level and swinging an arc with it to the same port and starboard shrouds. If the mast is off center, the halyard will appear shorter on one side. (Under sail in a breeze something has to give and the mast will inevitably fall off a bit to leeward.)

## Tuning Your Rig

Then start with the lower shrouds. When tuning, always begin with the lowers, and don't move on until that section of mast is vertical. Think of single-spreader rigs as two distinct masts, and double-spreader rigs as three distinct masts. With the lower shrouds, it's best to begin with the forward lowers, if any, then move to the after lowers. When the bottom section of the mast is vertical amidships and all lower shrouds are equally tensioned—the two-inch rule (or 20% rule) applies here as well—move to the upper shrouds and proceed in similar fashion. Again, the upper shrouds should have equal tension. At this stage, they should also have the same tension as all the lower shrouds.

Finally, be sure the spreaders are holding the upper shrouds securely. A spreader must bisect the angle of the shroud—in other words, the angles formed by the spreader and shroud above and below the spreader must be equal. If not, the load on the spreader will be uneven, putting strain on the spreader. Like the mast, the spreader is very strong under compression when the force is directed down its length. Now tape or otherwise secure the spreader to the shroud.

Fine-tuning must take place under sail. Fifteen knots of apparent wind is ideal. (Too little wind and the rig may not show a tendency to bend; too much and you may have difficulty making fine adjustments.) Hoist the largest headsail the boat can carry under the conditions, and put her hard on the wind. Trim the sails hard, let the boat settle in the groove, then sight up the mast. One of the mast configurations shown here may be evident. Simply follow the instructions under the configuration that most matches what you see, easing the sheets off completely to remove the tension from the rig before making adjustments.

There is one important thing to remember about fine-tuning: If you make a mistake, go back to the beginning.

Again, start with the lower shrouds, and then, when the lower section of the mast is aligned, move to the uppers. After each series of adjustments, trim the sails hard and bring the boat back up close-hauled. If the mast looks straight, come about and sail close-hauled on the opposite tack until you can determine whether the mast is straight or not. If not, make the necessary adjustments.

Ordinarily, unless the mast has a considerable bend in it, your adjustments will be no more than a few turns of the turnbuckle. Remember

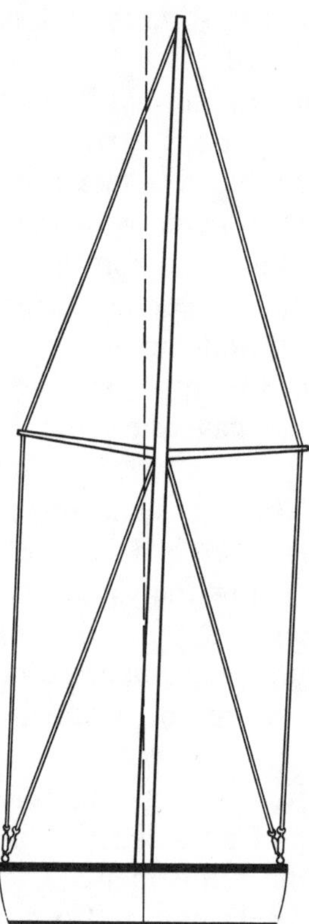

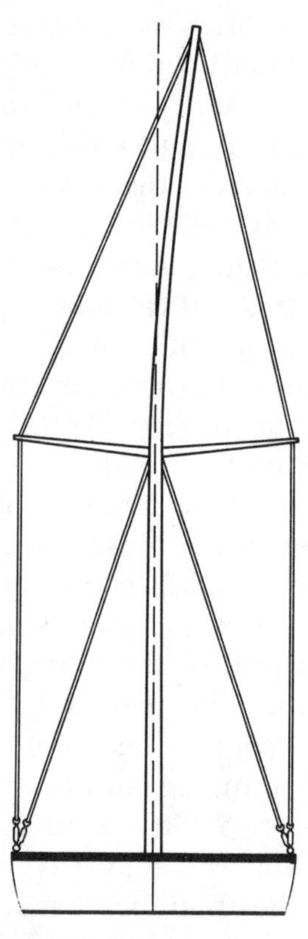

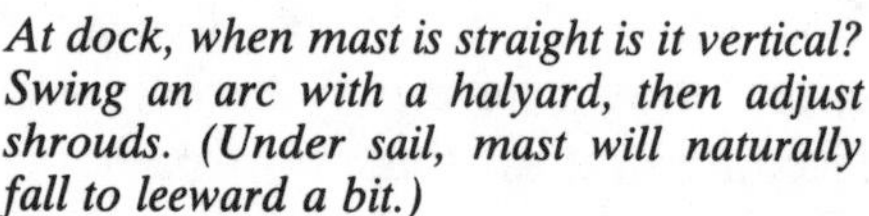

*At dock, when mast is straight is it vertical? Swing an arc with a halyard, then adjust shrouds. (Under sail, mast will naturally fall to leeward a bit.)*

*Lower shrouds seem fine—the problem lies with the uppers. Ease the starboard upper. If necessary, tighten port upper. Then tack to check results.*

the initial tensioning rule: Though cruising rigs can be tensioned to 25 percent of their breaking strength, don't go over that figure, and it's best to stay under 25 percent. Tuning is as much a process of loosening turnbuckles as it is of tightening them.

Note that the leeward shrouds will have reduced tension, particularly when the boat is close-hauled in a strong breeze. This is as it should be. But the leeward shrouds should not be slack. There is some difference of opinion about this point. Some authorities recommend that the leeward shrouds of their own rigs have appreciable tension at all times. Chuck Poindextor of Sound Rigging Services in Essex, Conn., suggests that leeward shrouds can be slack. Certainly there should not be enough slack

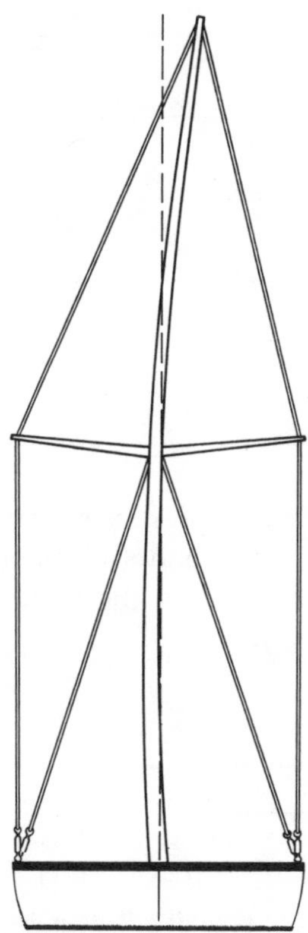

*Lower mast has too much compression. East port lower. Check starboard lower. If upper mast is still bent, see above, right. Then tack and check.*

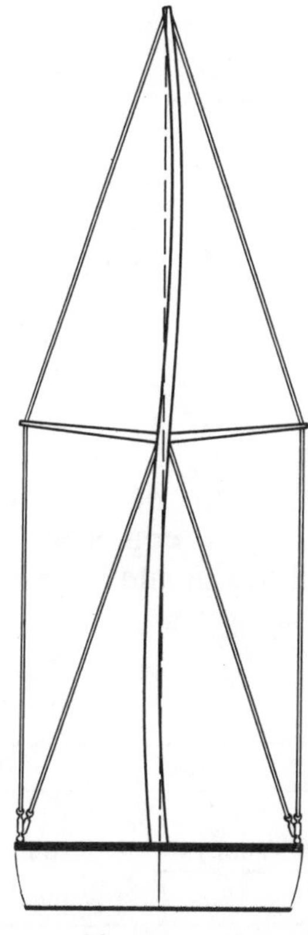

*Both upper and lower mast have too much compression. Ease port lower and port upper; also check starboard lower—it may need easing.*

to allow the rig to slop around in light air and a confused sea.

Rigs, like pianos, have a way of coming untuned after a time. The wire rope will stretch to a small degree, and the chainplates may settle, particularly with new rigging. You will want to retune a *new* boat after about fifty hours. Examine the mast regularly on both tacks during the season, and retune accordingly.

When you are convinced the rig is properly tuned, insert cotter pins in the turnbuckles and spread them about 10°. Install chafing sleeves over them or tape the pins. Be sure the spreader still bisects the upper shroud angle, and that it is securely fastened to the shroud.

*—Tom Parrett*

# FIRE EXTINGUISHERS

UNIT TYPE CAPACITY LOCATION DATES SERVICED

1. ______________________________

2. ______________________________

3. ______________________________

4. ______________________________

5. ______________________________

6. ______________________________

Mark locations of fire extinguishers, plus location of remote triggering devices if so equipped. Number according to schedule above. Fire extinguisher should be inspected and serviced at least at the beginning of each boating season.

| Type B Extinguisher Sizes | | | | | | |
|---|---|---|---|---|---|---|
| Classifications | | Foam | Carbon dioxide | Dry chemical | Halon 1301 | Halon 1211 |
| Type | Size | gallons | pounds | pounds | pounds | pounds |
| B | I | 1¾ | 4 | 2 | 2½ | 2½ |
| B | II | 2½ | 15 | 10 | — | — |
| B | III | 12 | 35 | 20 | — | — |

Note: Halon 1211 units of sizes greater than 9 pounds are not approved by USCG.

Listed above are fire extinguishers approved by the Coast Guard for use on boats. The B classification indicates these will put out flammable liquid fires, and the fire-fighting capacity is rated by the Coast Guard in sizes I, II, and III; a B-I extinguisher, for example, can be completely discharged in only 8 to 20 seconds. See pages 88-90 for information on the characteristics of the various types of extinguishing systems.

______________________________

______________________________

# SAFETY/SAFETY/SAFETY

## Safety Standards

Owning a boat is one of the few remaining kinds of personal freedom. You don't need an operator's license for pleasure boating. Safety "regulations" are minimal for excellent reasons. So safety is up to the boat owner.

In this chapter we look at some of the details of standards for the mechanical condition of boats and equipment. To be sure, most of the basics in other chapters affect safety. Properly tuned and maintained rigging rarely breaks. Properly installed fuel systems and engines don't have fires.

First, a reminder about the Coast Guard and other government standards: they are absolutely the minimum. This is not a criticism. Most people who know boating, including the Coast Guard, refrain from asking for legislation on every last detail of boats. This is because the sizes and types of boats vary widely, and because the uses and the waters they are operated upon vary much more widely than conditions encountered by motor vehicles. Also, in the field of boating, voluntary standards, drawn up by experts, are technically excellent. All you have to do is know about them and apply them to your particular boat and your particular boating activity.

Later in this section there is technical information on Coast Guard requirements for fire extinguishers and life preservers. Most well-found boats have more fire extinguishing equipment than the legal minimum. Availability in various parts of the boat is one key. In some cases, the ability to completely extinguish a fairly large fire, or the desire to have automatic compartment extinguishers is the reason. And a third reason is one founded on other people's experience: you can use up a small extinguisher putting out a small galley fire in a few seconds. If you have spares you can safely continue your voyage. Too, someday a boat docked next to yours may catch fire, and that's when extra extinguishers are invaluable.

Needless to say, proper installations and proper procedures will come very close to making your boat fire-proof. When you read the information in this section about fire extinguishers, remember that it is also background about the types of fires.

In many cases a marine insurance company can and will provide a good check on safety standards. Often premiums are reduced for special reasons such as automatic fire systems or that the owner has taken recognized courses in boat operation.

## Underwriters' Laboratories

Among the organizations that are involved with setting applicable safety standards are the National Fire Protection Association, Underwriters' Laboratories, and the American Boat and Yacht Council, as well as the U.S. Coast Guard. In large part these various standards are for the guidance of naval architects, boat manufacturers, and boat yards that install new engines or add fuel tanks or major equipment. However, the boat owner is well advised to be familiar with requirements or desirable standards. Among the most important are: galley stoves and fuel systems; electrical, including protection against lightning; and engines, including fuel tanks and lines. Most of the key points on recommended standards are in this book. The complete standards, including details on the proper operation of the systems, are obtainable from the American Boat and Yacht Council, at P.O. Box 806, 190 Ketcham Avenue, Amityville, N.Y. 11701. Their telephone number is: (516) 598-0550.

## American Boat and Yacht Council

Note: whether you buy a boat new or used, it will not necessarily already conform to all the desirable standards. The standards are upgraded from time to time. A professional survey is often desirable. Established yacht broker firms in your area can often supply you with the names of reputable, competent surveyors.

## Fire Extinguishers

Extinguishers carry a designation indicating the type of fire which they are designed to fight; the only ones that meet legal requirements for minimum equipment on boats are Class B units capable of extinguishing flammable liquid fires.

There are four types of extinguishing agents used in Class B units: dry chemical, carbon dioxide, foam and Halon. All except foam can be used on Class C (electrical) fires, but foam can be used on Class A (wood, paper, cloth) fires, as can some multipurpose dry chemicals.

**Dry chemical extinguishers.** An inert gas under pressure discharges a powder quite similar to baking soda. This triggers a chemical reaction that slows combustion and extinguishes the fire. A gauge or indicator shows that normal pressure exists within the tank. Spare cylinders can be screwed onto the discharge nozzle assembly, replacing an exhausted tank. There are some units you can refill and recharge yourself.

Some dry chemical extinguishers manufactured before June 1, 1965 do not have gauges. These are acceptable as legal equipment as long as they are in good condition; their state of fill must be checked by careful weighing.

## Fire Extinguishers

**Carbon dioxide ($CO_2$) extinguishers** leave no residue and cause no harm to engines when they are discharged. As an engine cannot burn carbon dioxide, it stops quickly when $CO_2$ is drawn into the cylinders. Extinguisher contents are checked by weight against a figure stamped on or near the valve.

**Foam,** although approved for marine extinguishers, is seldom used because of the mess it creates. If drawn into an engine intake, it may be necessary to do considerable disassembly for adequate cleaning. Underwriters Laboratories no longer lists new foam extinguishers.

**Halon** is a colorless, odorless gas that stops fire by chemical action. An engine will continue to run if Halon is discharged in its compartment, and if the engine is not immediately shut down it will pull so much of the extinguishing agent out of the compartment that the fire may flash back. It's best to rig an automatic system to kill the ignition as soon as a fixed Halon extinguisher is triggered. The main safety feature of the Halon 1301 is that humans can breathe it, unlike $CO_2$.

## Coast Guard Requirements

All extinguishers designed to meet legal requirements for marine use must be approved by a nationally recognized testing institution such as Underwriters Laboratories and by the U.S. Coast Guard. The Coast Guard rates extinguishers by fire-fighting capacity in sizes I, II and III (see Table on page 86). UL-approved extinguishers may also carry a designation that is a firefighting capacity rating, such as "1-A, 10-B:C." The number indicates the area, in square feet, an *experienced* fire fighter could be expected to put out.

Location of portable extinguishers is important. Whenever your fire alarm sounds, or you spot a fire in a non-monitored location, you want a portable extinguisher within reach, no matter where you are on your boat. You probably will wind up with two or more units than required by law. Install your extinguishers at each helm station, in the galley alongside (but not behind) the stove and in each cabin. For fuel and engine compartments, extinguishers must be *outside* the compartments where you can get at them.

Where primary access to an engine compartment is from above, National Fire Protection Association standards require that extinguisher discharge be possible from a point outside the compartment, into the area immediately surrounding the engine, without opening the primary access hatch.

Mount all extinguishers at least 2 inches above any deck or other surface where water might collect, to avoid corrosion of the cylinder base.

On many extinguishers, the pull ring that acts as a safety catch must be pulled out with the left hand, or you need to reach around awkwardly with the right hand to pull it while you hold the cylinder in your left hand. You and your regular crew should practice removing extinguishers from brackets and getting set to operate them.

Fixed systems should be automatically operated, backed up with manual releases at each helm station. You may spot a fire before a sensor sounds an alarm and triggers the system. Sensors are set to react when temperatures reach 165 to 190°F (74 to 88°C), and since heat rises, they should be mounted above any possible combustion source. Make sure they are secure from knocks or vibration that could cause malfunction.

When an automatic system is triggered, such as Fike's FiQuench (Halon) or Kidde's $CO_2$ type, don't immediately open the engine hatch to check its operation. You would be introducing fresh oxygen into the compartment, reducing the effectiveness of the system's extinguishing agent.

When you need to use portable extinguishers, aim at the base of the flames, and rapidly sweep the extinguisher back and forth, starting at the edge of the fire nearest you and working back. If additional extinguishers can be brought to bear, so much the better, as the time to completely discharge a B-I unit runs from only 8 to 20 seconds.

It may be possible to maneuver the boat to help in fighting a fire. Even stopping the boat helps to reduce wind that fans flames; turn the boat so the wind is behind you as you use the extinguisher, if possible, and if the fire is in the bow or stern, this will help keep the blaze from spreading to other parts of the boat.

## EPIRB

**EPIRB.** An EPIRB will broadcast distress signals on 121.5 and 243 MHz, the international distress frequencies monitored by aircraft. Ideally, its range is about 200 miles, but after knocking around a boat for a time, a more realistic range is 100 miles. At 60°F, one should broadcast for about 8 days, but range will drop to about 50 miles at the end. You can extend its life—and range—by carrying a small solar panel with converter to keep it humming when its batteries would fail.

The effectiveness of an EPIRB depends on its being picked up by a civil or military airplane. A commercial airliner is the best bet, but airlines tend to fly in tightly controlled air traffic corridors, and you stand the best chance of being heard if you are within 100 miles of these routes.

As you might guess, EPIRB stands for Emergency Position Indicating Radio Beacon.

# SAFETY/SAFETY/SAFETY

## Fueling Procedures

The following sequence of fueling procedures for gasoline-powered boats is based on recommendations of the Marine Division of Underwriters' Laboratories.

Before taking on fuel:

- Properly moor boat at fuel dock.
- Prohibit smoking on board or in vicinity.
- Shut down engines.
- Extinguish galley flames.
- Close all ports, windows, doors, hatches.
- Have a filled extinguisher handy.

While fueling:

- Make sure no fuel gets below decks, except into tanks.
- Maintain metal-to-metal contact between nozzle and fill pipe.
- Do not completely fill tanks; avoid gasoline flow through vent tubes.

After fueling:

- Secure fill cap.
- Wipe up all spillage and properly dispose of rags in containers ashore.
- Open all ports, doors, hatches.
- Ventilate bilge area at least five minutes.
- Be sure all enclosed spaces are completely free of gasoline odors before starting engines or lighting burners. Use your nose; don't rely on fume detectors alone.

Never fuel at night except under well-lighted conditions.

## New Mandatory Visual Distress Signals

Boats are required to have appropriate visual distress signals when in "coastal waters"—defined as the Great Lakes and the territorial seas of the United States, and the bays and sounds that empty into those waters.

Rivers, inside of a line drawn tangent to their headlands, are not subject to these new requirements unless the width across the river's mouth is more than two miles. Then, the rules apply on that river up to a point where it first narrows to a width of two miles.

Boats 16 feet or more in length, and boats of any size carrying six or fewer paying passengers, must carry visual distress signals of an "approved type" suitable for both day and night use. Boats less than 16 feet in length, when used between sunset and sunrise, must carry approved nighttime signals. Exceptions are made for craft competing in races, marine regattas, etc.; for manually propelled craft; and for sailboats under 26 feet in length, without machinery, and of completely open construction.

Typical acceptable signals include hand-held and floating orange smoke signals, projected red flares of both the aerial rocket and parachute type, orange flags of specific design with round and square black marks, and electrical signal lights that automatically flash S-O-S—three dots, three dashes, three dots. Except for the flag and automatic electric light, three of any type signal must be carried to meet the requirements. Note carefully that *hand-held red flares are now included in the list of acceptable types of visual distress signals.*

While there is no prohibition to such flares being on board a boat, there is no requirement either, and all boatmen should be fully aware of their inherent dangers. The best hand-held flares are drip free. Beware of personal burns or possible fire risks.

The effective date for the new visual distress signal requirements is January 1, 1981. Specifications and testing procedures have been published and it is anticipated that Coast Guard approved devices will be available before the deadline date. Until July 1, 1982, existing visual distress signals or the aerial or parachute red flare and hand-held or floating orange smoke types will be accepted. In addition, there are similar types of visual distress signals approved by the Coast Guard for use on larger vessels which are readily available. These are acceptable for smaller boats.

## PFD's

By law, there must be an approved wearable PFD for each person on board any boat 16 feet or more in length, plus one throwable device. Under this size, there must be one wearable or throwable type for each person in the boat. Each water skier being towed counts as a person in the boat. There are four types of PFDs that meet these legal requirements:

**Type I Life Preservers.** These must provide more than 20 pounds of buoyancy and turn an unconscious person to a vertical or slightly backward position with the face out of water. Note that when a person is in the water, most of the weight is supported by the water itself; the buoyancy figures given with PFDs indicate the amount of weight they should support out of the water. Tests show that buoyancy requirements for adults range from 7¼ pounds for a small woman to 17½ pounds for a large man.

Life preservers must be international orange in color, with kapok or fibrous glass flotation material encased in sealed plastic film covers under fabric. If the bib type, flotation material is unicellular foam sections of specified shape sewn into cloth or dipped in vinyl. The bib type must have a slit all the way down the front and adjustable body straps. There are two sizes (plainly marked on the preservers): "Adult," for persons 90 pounds or more in weight, and "Child," for persons under this weight.

All life preservers carry a Coast Guard approval number, the date and place of inspection, the inspector's initials and the phrase "Approved for use on all vessels and motor boats."

## Life Preservers

**Type II Buoyant Vests.** These must be capable of turning an unconscious person face up and provide at least 15½ pounds of positive buoyancy. Buoyant vests have the same requirements for materials as life preservers, but they are smaller, more comfortable to wear, and may be any color. They are made in adult, medium and small sizes (the latter two for youngsters), and they carry a Coast Guard approval number but no individual inspector's initials. Stow them where they can be grabbed in any sort of emergency. Any PFD stowage spot should be clearly labeled, and as stated all the PFDs should be international orange. It's the most visible color under most sea conditions.

You and your crew should practice donning the devices, both in the boat and in the water. In the water it may only be possible to hang onto the PFD; try to find the position that is least tiring and provides the most support. The most important thing is to *wear* the PFDs whenever weather is rough, or any sort of dangerous situation might develop. Don't worry about your "image." A capsize or knockdown can toss a boat's occupants into the sea with no time to grab a PFD, let alone put it on.

**Type II Flotation Jackets.** Material is a flexible, unicellular foam which may be a polyvinyl chloride or polyethylene type, or a similar closed-cell foam that will not absorb water even if the outer protective shell is damaged. Stearns' "Aquafoam" and the Uniroyal "Ensolite" used by a number of PFD manufacturers are examples.

**Type III Flotation Coats.** These must provide at least 15½ pounds of positive buoyancy, but do not turn an unconscious person face-up. They may be any color, and unicellular foam is the flotation material. All carry a Coast Guard approval number.

In cooler weather the flotation coats make a lot of sense; they look good both afloat and ashore. In the water the foam acts as insulation that retards loss of body heat (hypothermia), a process that is 25 times faster than loss of body heat to air. Some Type III coats are designed and sold as "survival jackets," with special features to protect vulnerable heat loss areas such as the head, neck, thoracic duct region along the spine, lateral thorax along the sides of the chest, and groin.

The Stearns Offshore Survival Jacket, for example, has an inner lining of stretch neoprene that hugs the body and acts as a wet suit to minimize heat loss, plus an insulation-lined hood, high collar, and elasticized wrist bands to help keep water out of sleeves.

Ultimate survival suits are much like oversize wet suits. These enclose the body fully, including feet and hands. Two manufacturers are Bailey Suit Co. of Fortuna, Calif. and Imperial Mfg. Co. of Bremerton, Wash.

**Type IV Flotation Cushions.** These are throwable devices, although the cushions can count toward the one-PFD-person requirement on boats less than 16 feet in length. Cushion material may be kapok, fibrous glass or unicellular foam, with the kapok or glass sealed in plastic film covers. Cushions must have Coast Guard Approval number on the tag to be legal, and they will carry the warning: "Do not wear on back."

**Type IV Life Rings and Horseshoes.** Life rings come in 18-, 20-, 24- and 30-inch diameters, with the smallest one legal only on boats that do not carry passengers for hire. Rings must provide at least 20 pounds buoyancy. The flotation material may be cork or balsa wood covered with fabric, or unicellular foam with special surface treatment. These devices carry the Coast Guard approval number, inspection date and place and inspector's initials. Color may be white or international orange, and the boat's name may be painted on the ring.

Horseshoes are made of unicellular foam, with a cover of nylon or similar hard-wearing material not affected by moisture or mildew. Units of this type must provide 32 pounds or more positive buoyancy. As with life rings, there is a Coast Guard approval number and inspection information.

Horseshoe rings are the favorite with the sailing crowd; life rings are found most often on powerboats. In any sort of sea, it's difficult to get head and shoulders through a ring—it's best to grab hold and hang onto it. The horseshoe is preferred on sailboats because there's greater likelihood of a man-overboard situation, and the victim, possibly burdened by foul weather gear, is likely to be in the water longer before the boat can maneuver back for the pickup. There are quick-release brackets for horseshoes; a man-overboard pole tied to the PFD triggers the release when the pole is tossed into the sea. The soft, flexible construction of the horseshoe makes it relatively easy to slip under the shoulders in the water.

## Survival Gear

SURVIVAL SUITS

| QUANTITY SIZE | LOCATION | DATES INSPECTED |
|---|---|---|
| | | |
| | | |

## Life Rafts

Life Rafts

| UNIT | CAPACITY | DATES INSPECTED |
|---|---|---|
| | | |
| | | |

# FIRST AID

## by Henry J. Wharton, M.D.

### Pain

Our body's best friend is usually pain, which indicates that something is out of order. It is the absence of pain in such deadly diseases as cancer, diabetes and tuberculosis that makes the initial diagnosis so difficult. Pain is, therefore, a valuable sign that should not be ignored.

### Fever

Fever in itself is not a disease but an indication that our body is trying to fight some invading germs that have no business where they are. An infection with no fever reaction is often more serious than one that produces a healthy elevation of body temperature.

The absence of exact knowledge of the mechanism that generates fever has led to the production of a rich mythology. To clarify the many misconceptions: 98.6° does not constitute normal body temperature; it rather indicates the upper limit of normal temperature. Everything below is perfectly normal and not "subnormal." Above 98.6°, fever begins. The questions then arise of what to do about it, and at what point we should intervene. It will be helpful to remember that small children may run high temperatures on the slightest provocation. Nevertheless, fever should be stopped from going higher than 100-101°.

The best way to stop fever is, of course, to take aspirin or any of the many aspirin combinations or substitutes that appear nightly on your TV screen. If fever reaches 103°, sponge baths with a mixture containing 50% alcohol and 50% water should be administered every 15-20 minutes. This should bring the fever down within one to two hours. However, if the sponge baths fail to lower the temperature, a cold-water enema (ice-cold, if obtainable) repeated at half-hour intervals will do it without fail. At no point is a fever a cause for worry because it is always possible to bring it down. The question is only how far one wants to go.

By the end of your cruise you will be as brown as a berry, but don't try to get all the sun on your first day out. Because of its reflection, sunlight is ten times stronger on the water than ashore. Therefore, expose your tender winter skin just a few minutes initially, then cover yourself with one of the many sunscreens available or spend the rest of the day in the shade.

## FIRST AID

**Suntan and Sunburn**

Once skin gets burned it is even more imperative to keep out of the sun. Therefore, a sunscreen has therapeutic value. Clothing should be as light and loose as possible—pajamas are usually the least irritating. It is probably of some value to remember that even the fiercest sunburn is usually not more than a first degree burn and that after 24-48 hours, the worst suffering is over. This overall view naturally does not impress the burn-sufferer who would like some relief then and there. Fortunately a number of creams and sprays are on the market whose trade names usually contain the syllable "cain" thus indicating that they are related to Novacain, the excellent local anesthetic. Consequently, their application gives some relief but cannot be compared with not getting burned in the first place.

**Hemorrhage**

One of the most frightening occurrences in life is bleeding, regardless of its source. Since our body runs on only six quarts of the precious stuff, its loss ought to be stopped as soon as possible. However, many hours have been wasted learning the points of application of tourniquets. The results were often disastrous because entire limbs were destroyed by the lack of circulation. Fortunately, our body in its miraculous ways has the capacity to let our blood clot when it comes in contact with air or a cut in our skin. This depends naturally on the size of the cut. A small cut will stop bleeding by itself within a few minutes, but a larger one needs some assistance in the form of pressure applied directly on top of the cut. This pressure may consist of a few gauze squares or a clean rag held tightly in place by our hands or with the help of an elastic bandage. Either way as long as it remains undisturbed this will stop even the most frightful looking hemorrhage within minutes.

This principle applies also to nosebleeds which in general enjoy a considerable amount of folklore such as where cold compresses should be applied: the back of the neck, the top of the forehead, etc. Actually all they take is a wick, fashioned out of cotton and introduced into the nostril, followed by steady pressure against the afflicted side of the nose. The trick is not to remove the wick too early to check whether the bleeding has really stopped. This will start the bleeding without fail and the same procedure has to be repeated.

**Seasickness**

Although the true location of the center for seasickness (if such a thing should exist) is still being debated, with some placing it in the nerves of the stomach and others attributing it purely to the mind, it helps to take both views into account and treat both areas simultaneously. Thus the words seasickness, mal-de-mer, vomiting, nausea, etc. are strictly to be omitted from the sea-going vocabulary. Motion sickness comfort bags, so liberally provided by the airline industry, should be banned from sight and reach.

On the other hand anybody who turns suddenly green and very quiet should be handed without discussion a Dramamine or similar tablet by the skipper and should be kept busy with chores. Crewmembers who become very sleepy from their medication may lie down on the decks, but not below. Guests known to be subject to motion sickness should take their medication one hour before sailing time.

*After these general remarks I would like to pay some attention to specific organs and what may befall them on a cruise. To do this in a more or less systematic fashion I shall begin with the head and work my way anatomically down.*

## The Head

The forceful collision between our head and a firm object like a jibing boom or a cabin sole in a precipitous descent down the companionway may be unpleasant, to say the least. However, the resulting unconsciousness is not necessarily dangerous, provided the stricken crewmember wakes up within a reasonable time. (Persisting unconsciousness or its recurrence after a lucid interval or bleeding from the ears, mouth or nose are ominous signs requiring hospitalization as soon as feasible.) The nausea and/or vomiting or headaches will gradually subside. To shorten the recovery time the crewmember should be made to lie down flat. The swelling at the point of impact enjoys a rich folklore regarding its treatment, but all it really needs are cold compresses or icebags to keep further swelling under control.

## Eyes

On a boat the eyes may be exposed to one of two emergencies. The first is a foreign body, the other an inflammation of the conjunctiva, the fine membrane covering our eyes and eyelids. (Strangely enough, many times a sudden inflammation of the conjunctiva feels exactly like a foreign body.)

The removal of a foreign body is extremely simple if you were born with three hands: With the first you hold a matchstick horizontally in the crease of the upper lid, with the second you grasp the eyelashes and turn the upper lid over the matchstick inside out and with the third you take a wisp of cotton and wipe whatever was hiding under the upper lid away. Two-armed operators take a little longer but finally they manage too.

A serious warning: Removal of a foreign body embedded in the cornea (the glassy part in the center of the eye) belongs in the office of an ophthalmologist. Any attempt of removal will be resented by both the ophthalmologist as well as the cornea, because the cornea is even more sensitive than the eye-doctor, and may sustain permanent damage. Just put a drop of mineral oil in and tape the eye closed with Scotch tape and send your patient ashore. He'll be back in an hour and eternally grateful to you.

For an inflammation of the conjunctiva there are an abundant number of eye-ointments or drops, all containing either sulfacetamide or Neomycin, with or without Hydrocortisone. Whatever you choose will do the trick and usually the worst inflammation is painless within a few hours and healed in two to three days.

No doubt, we live in an unfriendly world full of germs and viruses who would have eaten us alive long ago if our body did not have an excellent shield to protect us: Our skin which is impervious to all germs as long as it remains unbroken. But, like all heroes in history, our body—pardon the pun—has its Achilles heel: the throat, entrance to our respiratory organs.

## Ear, Nose and Throat

Naturally, it is plastered with lymphoid tissue where the lymphocytes, our little defenders, come from, but this constant battle between attackers and defenders is a painful process, especially for us, the battleground in the middle.

There are many hundreds of different germs ready to do us in, but, luckily, medical science has an adequate number of antibiotics to help us in our struggle. Because, if the battle is not won here, in the throat, it will be continued farther down, in the windpipe, in the bronchial tubes, in the ear canals and in the lungs.

Naturally, it would be quite preposterous to expect the skipper to carry all possible antibiotics in his medicine chest and it is our good fortune that there are some antibiotics with a broad enough range to protect us against the majority of the most common invaders: the tetracyclines and the semisynthetic penicillins. Both are available as capsules and, for children, as syrups, and, if taken early enough in case of a throat infection, are capable of preventing most complications. Let me add to this the therapeutic gem that 80% of all earaches are caused by congestion of the nasal end of the Eustachian tube and therefore quickly curable by nosedrops and sprays.

## Toothaches

Most toothaches result from food particles, especially sweets, being stuck in a tooth cavity. Therefore a thorough brushing and rinsing will usually remove the offenders and terminate this emergency. A visit to the dentist before the cruise is an advisable ounce of prevention.

## The Chest

1) ***Cough*** is usually a complication of a respiratory infection and serves the body to expel a good number of the germs and the debris of the battlefield. Therefore not every cough should be treated with suppressants, only those hard, dry coughs that keep you awake in the night; most doctors have their favorites. The essential trick is to remember to treat the respiratory infection at the same time with antibiotics.

2) ***Pain*** in the chest is, like neck pain, often caused by exposure to draft and spasms in the muscles of the chest. (See also Neck.)

Not very much can go wrong with a neck on a boat: It can be exposed

## The Neck

to a cold draft so that its muscles get into a spasm which is painful like a pain in the neck, but not serious. Heat and gentle message, preferably by the prettiest girl aboard, will soon take care of it. "Swollen glands" are usually a symptom that some infection is going on in the throat. Treat that and they will disappear.

Other chestpains are often located "below the heart" and are usually caused by accumulation of gas in the stomach or the transverse colon. The personality of the sufferer from this kind of pain often tells the story: They occur in nervous, tense and sensitive people who are an easy prey to their emotions, to aggravation and excitement. Removal of the gas is desirable but not always easily accomplished. (Try belching, passing gas and going to the toilet.)

Heartburn usually takes place directly under the breastbone and is produced by gastric acid that for one reason or another got into the esophagus (gullet) which is not made for it. A large dose of an antacid will take care of it.

Pain caused by a disorder of the heart itself is usually not located where the heart is but under the upper breastbone and radiates down the left arm feeling like a giant hand squeezing the heart. It may last just a few seconds and will make the stricken do exactly what his heart needs: keep absolutely still until it passes. This is angina and most angina sufferers know about their condition and carry tiny tablets with them. It is not very likely for anyone to have his first angina attack on a boat.

If however this attack persists in all severity for several hours, causing the outbreak of a cold sweat, you may witness the most serious of all emergencies on a boat, a coronary thrombosis. Speed without panic is of the essence. Let your patient sit where he is comfortable; don't force him to lie down; don't make him smell your aromatic spirits; don't make him drink anything hot or cold or alcoholic, but quietly summon the Coast Guard. Give them the exact position of your boat, explain to them the serious nature of your patient's illness, ask them to bring oxygen along and transport your man to the nearest hospital. You will be pleasantly surprised by the helpfulness and efficiency of our Coast Guard.

(A word of consolation: Should it turn out that your diagnosis was wrong and your patient had nothing but an unusually severe gaspocket remember that 85% of us professionals with medical licenses would have made the same mistake—this being the number of "coronaries" that on further testing dissolve into thin air.)

Below the diaphragm a few conditions exist which, thanks to our intricate anatomy, make themselves felt in the chest. Aside from these the most feared is appendicitis. As everybody's grandmother knows, appendicitis is characterized by pain on the right side and has to be treated by an appendectomy within the hour. Appendectomies on the high seas performed with a steak knife and kitchen spoon are adored by the Mod Squad crowd but frowned upon by surgeons who cannot trim a toenail without their staff of residents, interns and scrubnurses.

Be that as it may, the wise skipper will be well advised to shun such seagoing antics and to bring his crewmember with appendicitis ashore as fast as possible.

## The Abdomen

However, before any such drastic steps are taken it should be pointed out that even the best-meaning grandmothers may be wrong and not everything that hurts on the right side is appendicitis. To save many a cruise from an embarrassing and usually not inexpensive excursion to some emergency ward or surgeon ashore let me enumerate all the right-sided abdominal pains that are *not* appendicitis:

1) All pains that are on the left side as well as on the right. (They can be quite severe and point to some goings on within the intestines—most likely what is generally known as "intestinal flu." More about that later.)
2) Pains that start suddenly, lightning-like, on the right side. (Most likely an accumulation of gas that inflates that part of the gut more than others.)
3) Pains that are accompanied by diarrhea. (Again most probably some variation of a viral intestinal flu).
4) Pains that are accompanied by burning at, or frequency of, urination. (Obviously an infection of the bladder, working its way up to the right kidney.)
5) Pains in young ladies occurring exactly at midpoint between two menstrual periods. This is caused by ovulation and may even produce a little blood.

Real appendicitis begins usually with pain around the bellybutton and with nausea. This is a steady, not a crampy pain that gradually becomes more severe and slowly shifts down to the right side (to the center of a line from the navel to the uppermost point of the pelvis). There is vomiting and, most commonly, constipation. The muscles of the abdomen try to protect this inflamed side against any pressure from outside, and stiffen noticeably when examined.

Other intestinal diseases sail under at least as many names as there are germs causing them: There is "food poisoning," "the 24 hour flu," the "stomach bug," "dysentery" or "the runs," "ptomaine poisoning," "acute gastro-enteritis." More severe forms are called: "la turista" and "Montezuma's revenge." Whatever the name, the principle is the same: a viral infection of a part of the alimentary canal, the symptoms depending on which area is most severely infected: if the stomach and upper intestines are predominantly involved, vomiting may occur often quite uncontrollably. If the lower intestines are more affected, diarrhea will result. If both sets of symptoms prevail you may safely conclude that the entire works are in uproar. Severe fatigue and strange, uncommonly spicy foods often prepare the gound by lowering our resistance—which is why the Mexican variety is so very vicious.

## Vomiting

The treatment, although simple, does not enjoy great popularity because the first step is to withhold all food and all fluids, in order to put the entire gastro-intestinal tract at complete rest. There is even some logic in this cruel madness because if you give your patient two spoonsfuls of water and he throws up a pint you need no computer to tell you he is dehydrated. This, however, is only the first and most elementary step. Now you go to your medicine chest and work the miracles of modern medicine: There are a number of excellent preparations available which will stop vomiting very shortly; they come in form of tablets, liquids, suppositories and injections. Oral medication is, of course, out of the questions because you will get it returned in no time. Thus, stick to rectal suppositories or, if you know how to use syringe and needle, an injection. This will stop in no time at all any vomiting, but not the diarrhea. For that you use a tiny tablet of Lomotil (after the vomiting has reliably stopped) and the acute phase of your illness is over. (In cases of severe tropical diarrhea you may have to resort to "Deodorized Tincture of Opium," which is not as interesting or addicting as the name may make you believe. You can't groove on it, but 10 to 15 drops in some water will stop the most resistant diarrhea.)

All this is, for a few days at least, to be followed by an extremely light and bland diet, dry toast, cooked cereals, mashed potatoes, boiled rice or pureed vegetables until the intestinal revolution is over and more stable bowel functions have returned.

At this point an often neglected matter should be mentioned: The change from a balanced diet to the often canned food afloat is apt to produce constipation in some people. I can however think of no civilized way for the skipper to find out whether all his crewmembers have done their daily duty. But there are numerous mild bowel regulators available and they should have their place in the ship's medicine chest.

The last abdominal emergency deserving mention here is an acute infection of the urinary tract. This is painful and embarrassing because it burns and requires visits to the head every few minutes. Besides, it is one of the few conditions that may produce a real high fever. If no medication is available a generous flushing out of the plumbing with nothing fancier than water may arrest this condition mechanically. But I would not like to rely on it. One of the Azo-sulfas should be in the medicine chest and will provide prompt, although temporary relief. Caution: Don't get frightened, it colors your urine orange-red. This isn't blood, it's the medicine.

## Bones and Joints

Bones and joints are so well constructed that you could not break or dislocate them even if you tried with all your strength. But it can happen in an extraordinarily hard fall, therefore we'd better talk about it. Except for the shoulder no joint ever becomes dislocated in spite of the chiropractors' folklore. And most dislocated shoulders can be easily fixed by the following maneuver: Have your patient lie down and place your foot into his armpit—preferably after removing your sneaker. Grasp his hand firmly and exert a gentle, steadily increasing pull toward you until you feel, or hear, the shoulder snap into place. That's all. If you don't succeed have him see a surgeon.

In a fracture (Latin for broken bone) we have an occasion to watch the most miraculous capacity of our body to repair itself (which is more than can be said for a broken spar or a torn sail). All we have to do is provide complete immobility of the fragments, and within days little bone cells are growing across the gap. But since not all fractures are in perfect alignment and may require "setting" we'd better take the stricken crewmember ashore to a hospital with the necessary equipment. Fractures become painless as soon as we keep the broken ends from rubbing against each other. Therefore a well functioning splint is essential: A spare sail batten or a rolled up magazine, fastened with some adhesive (or electrical or Rip-stop tape) will provide an excellent temporary splint.

Broken ribs, too, will respond promptly to a tight strapping with whatever tape we have available. Thanks to the construction of our chestcage no further shoreside treatment will be necessary. See to it that during application of the strapping the chest is kept in fully exhaled position.

Tongue depressors, contrary to prevailing opinion do not make ideal splints for broken fingers. Fingerjoints are extremely sensitive to being placed on a straight splint and long after the broken bone has healed the joints will remain so stiff that the entire hand is not very useful. A much better way is to splint a broken finger around a bandage roll.

## The Skin

The skin is much more than a tight cover that holds our body with all its organs together. It is a living organ with many talents and many extreme sensitivities.

One of its talents is the capacity to regenerate itself and to grow over almost any size cut provided we keep it free from infection and bring the edges of the cut into close approximation. The thorough cleansing of the inside of a cut is not apt to increase the popularity of the skipper and if he is at all able to use a syringe and needle he would be well advised to inject some local anesthetic around the wound edges. After that he can proceed with the scrubbing of the wound. Use liquid soap, peroxide and finally one of the newer antiseptics. The cooperation and gratitude of the scrubbee will always be his.

Except for very deep cuts that require being sewn in layers from the bottom up, the sewing of every cut is one of those tribal rites we can dispense with, especially on a boat where none of the essential tools are available. We can do just as good a job of approximation by using strips of adhesive or any other good tape. Cover the works with a sterile dressing.

Besides its talents our skin has a number of weaknesses: It doesn't like being burned or scalded, it reacts furiously to poison ivy, jelly fish, Portuguese-Men-of-War, certain corals and medicines as well as foods our body is allergic to. It is helpless vis-à-vis infections once its protective uppermost layer has been removed.

## Burns

First degree burns have been dealt with under the heading of sunburn. (It is immaterial for our skin what we burn it with.) In a second degree burn our skin raises blisters and I would like to plead with the skipper to resist the temptation to prick these blisters open. They, too, constitute a layer of protection and will open by themselves as soon as the skin has had time enough to grow a new protective layer beneath the blister.

Too energetic cleansing should not be indulged in; just hold the burned part under running cold water which flushes most of the dirt away and at the same time provides a fair amount of local anesthesia. Then cover the burned part thickly with a good burn ointment to exclude all air (which causes most of the pain) and wrap it in sterile gauze. This sterile dressing should be left in place for several days until healing has at least started. If it should look dirty (which it soon will) just pile more sterile dressing on top but leave the original dressing alone.

A third degree burn (one where all layers of the skin are charred or cooked) belongs in the sterile environment of a hospital.

The skin eruptions following contact with poison ivy, jelly-fish, fire-coral or following ingestion of an allergenic food or medicine may yield to one of many sprays (like Rhulispray) or may require cold soothing compresses with oatmeal or starch. Scratching, although tempting and momentarily enormously satisfying, should be discouraged because in the long run the skin becomes increasingly more irritated.

Internal treatment with cortisone, although most successful in any of these conditions should not be attempted except under the guidance of an experienced physician.

# FIRST AID

Dr. Henry Wharton cruised with his family for many years aboard the beautiful Sparkman & Stephens sloop *Many Moons.* His sailing experienced matched his family medical experience in preparing this chapter.

## First Aid Supplies

## General Supplies

Cotton, 1 roll (sterile preferred)
Gauze pads, (sterile and non-sterile, sizes 3×3, 4×4)
"Kling" bandage rolls, 2″ wide. (Easier to use than ordinary bandage rolls)
Band-aids, 1 can assorted
Cotton tipped applicators, 1 bag
Adhesive tape, ½″ and 1″ rolls, one each (also very good to tape cotton pins)
Thermometer (oral)
Enema bag
Splinter forceps
Scissors
Epsom salts (for soaks)
Tincture of green soap, 2 oz. (to wash out wounds)
Peroxide 8 oz. (to clean out wounds, especially infected wounds.)
Alcohol (the least expensive rubbing alcohol)
Zephiran* 1 oz. (to sterilize wounds)
Uval* (excellent sunscreen)
Nupercainal cream* (for mile burns)
Rx Furacin soluble dressing* (for severe burns or infected skin areas)
Rx—Prescription required
*—Proprietary name

The duration, and distance away from hospitals, of your cruising govern your choice of specific medications and supplies that are carried aboard. If your doctor is a boating person, he or she will be better at listening to your request for prescription drugs to be carried "just in case." For a long offshore voyage, get *The Ship's Medicine Chest and Medical Aid at Sea.* It costs $10.25 and is published by the U.S. Department of Health and Welfare. Dr. Nicholas C. Leone's *Cruising Sailor's Medical Guide*, published by McKay, is another useful book. See also *Standard First Aid* and *Advanced First Aid*, published by the American Red Cross.

## Specific Medications

| INDICATION | NAME | STRENGTH | DOSAGE |
|---|---|---|---|
| Infections, sore throats, earaches, etc. | Tetracyclin Hcl. (Rx) | 250 mgm caps<br>125 mgm/tsp (liquid)<br>250 mgm/tsp | 1 capsule or 1 tsp every 4-6 hours |
| same | Ampicillin (Rx) | same | same |
| Urinary infections | Azo-Gantanol* (Rx) | 0.5Gm | 2 tablets twice daily |
| Colds, runny noses, earaches | Neo-synephrin* | ¼%-1% | 3-5 drops, every 3-4 hours |
| Pain, Fever | Aspirin, APCs* Anacin,* Empirin* | 5 Gr or 1¼ Gr (children) | 1-2 every 4 hours |
| Severe pain | Percodan* (Rx) | Full strength | 1 tablet every 6 hours |

| INDICATION | NAME | STRENGTH | DOSAGE |
|---|---|---|---|
| Seasickness | Dramamine* | Tablets: 50 mgm<br>Liquid: 12.5 mgm (children)<br>Vials for injection<br>50 mgm (Rx)<br>Suppositories 100 mgm (Rx) | 1 every 4 hours |
| Vomiting and nausea | Torecan* (Rx) | 10 mgm tablets<br>10 mgm vials<br>10 mgm suppositories | 1 oz. 3 times daily |
| same | Compazine* (Rx) | Tablets 5 & 10mgm<br>Vials (injection) 5mgm<br>Syrup (children) 5mgm/tsp<br>Suppositories: 2.5 & 5mgm | 5-10 mgm, 2, 3, or 4 times daily |
| Diarrhea | Lomotil* (Rx) | 2.5 mgm tablets<br>2.5 mgm/tsp of syrup | One to two 3-4 times daily |
| Same, not controllable by any amount of Lomotil | Deodorized Tincture of Opium (Rx) | ½ oz. | 10-15 drops in water 2-3 times daily |
| Heartburn, indigestion | Antacids, like Tums,* Gelusil* Maalox,* Mylanta* | Immaterial (Liquid more effective, tablets easy to carry around) | Any amount, until symptoms are relieved |
| Constipation, mild "bowel regulators" | Senokot,* Milk of Magnesia,* Agarol* | Immaterial | Follow instructions on bottle |
| Strong laxative | Citrate of Magnesia | Immaterial | Follow instructions |
| Local anesthetic | Xylocain (Rx) | 1% 30cc | |
| Syringes and needles | (Disposable) (Rx) | 2½ cc, gauge #17, 1" long | |

# ON KEEPING LOGS

There are many ways to keep a log, and like many of the other pleasures of boating, they are not usually involved in laws and regulations. Even the customs are changing.

Some boat owners are so electronically up to date that they keep a log by dictating into a portable tape recorder. "Buoy # 18 is abeam, and it is ten pm. The sea is calm, the sky is clear."

Others put clippings, snapshots, and little drawings by people they meet in faraway ports into part of their log books. This seems like such a good idea that we have provided special log pages in this book: for favorite recipes, and for children's signatures, notes or drawings.

Some people make their log book into a navigational record, to supplement the markings on their charts. Others mainly keep a diary of parties and other fun, guests, other boats met, and even warnings about restaurants where the chowder is only mediocre.

**Business Entertaining**

There are one or two legal points to make: if you have a radio-telephone and license, you already know you must keep a record of calls made and received. So the appropriate pages are in this book. If you use your boat for business entertaining, the guest record is helpful.

It is rare for a pleasureboat log book to end up in a courtroom. Conceivably one could . . . and if so there are one or two things to remember. In the old days the rough or deck log was kept in pencil . . . but the formal log was written in ink. More convincing to a jury. Numbered pages are more believable . . . no lawyer is likely to accuse you of having removed pages from the log. In one case, the cross-examination and the log itself revealed that the owner had kept no log the weeks before the accident . . . and none at any other time. His log pages were less convincing, of course.

In the words of Charles F. Chapman, the log book is the official record of your boat's cruise. The data therein forms an important accessory to piloting as well, not only on the particular cruise in question but for all other trips over the same or approximately the same routes. The data recorded in the log book also may be a contribution to the general fund of knowledge concerning waters used for cruising; therefore, the facts and figures entered in the log book should be accurate and conclusive. In the case of large sea-going vessels the entries in the log are frequently referred to as evidence in legal actions, and this can happen with smaller boats as well.

While there are numerous forms of log books available, most of these are not well suited. The log sheet shown with this chapter has been designed especially to meet the needs of both small and large cruising boats whose owners are interested in coastwise cruising and proper piloting. The column headings are self-explanatory and may be kept as completely as desired.

Naturally, and legally, the license for your boat, or the documentation papers, should be kept aboard at least while the boat is in the water. Papers pertaining to your radiotelephone license are required to be aboard. It is suggested that inside the cover of this book is a good place; alternatively a zip-lock plastic envelope makes a good container. You will need to show the papers if your boat is ever boarded by the Coast Guard, or in a case of a "courtesy inspection."

The details on your insurance policy can be kept on the fill-in page at the front of this book, including the agent's name and telephone number.

## Chart List

| Chart Number | Area | Date, latest corrections |
|---|---|---|

Chart List. Use this space to record charts.

# GUEST REGISTER

| Date and Port | Name and Home Address | Yacht Club |
|---|---|---|
| | | |
| | | |
| | | |
| | | |
| | | |
| | | |
| | | |
| | | |
| | | |
| | | |
| | | |
| | | |
| | | |
| | | |
| | | |
| | | |
| | | |
| | | |
| | | |
| | | |

# GUEST REGISTER

| Date and Port | Name and Home Address | Yacht Club |
|---|---|---|
| | | |
| | | |
| | | |
| | | |
| | | |
| | | |
| | | |
| | | |
| | | |
| | | |
| | | |
| | | |
| | | |
| | | |
| | | |
| | | |
| | | |
| | | |
| | | |
| | | |
| | | |

# GUEST REGISTER

| Date and Port | Name and Home Address | Yacht Club |
|---|---|---|
| | | |
| | | |
| | | |
| | | |
| | | |
| | | |
| | | |
| | | |
| | | |
| | | |
| | | |
| | | |
| | | |
| | | |
| | | |
| | | |
| | | |
| | | |
| | | |
| | | |
| | | |

# GUEST REGISTER

| Date and Port | Name and Home Address | Yacht Club |
|---|---|---|
| | | |
| | | |
| | | |
| | | |
| | | |
| | | |
| | | |
| | | |
| | | |
| | | |
| | | |
| | | |
| | | |
| | | |
| | | |
| | | |
| | | |
| | | |
| | | |
| | | |
| | | |

# CRUISING LOG

| Time | Place Abeam: Buoy, Landmark or Other | Distance off | COURSE TO NEXT OBJECTIVE | | | Motor R.P.M. |
|---|---|---|---|---|---|---|
| | | | Course Steered | Magnetic | Distance | |
| | | | | | | |
| | | | | | | |
| | | | | | | |
| | | | | | | |
| | | | | | | |
| | | | | | | |
| | | | | | | |
| | | | | | | |
| | | | | | | |
| | | | | | | |
| | | | | | | |
| | | | | | | |
| | | | | | | |
| | | | | | | |
| | | | | | | |
| | | | | | | |
| | | | | | | |
| | | | | | | |
| | | | | | | |

# CRUISING LOG

| Estimated Speed | Estimated Time to Next Objective | Actual Time Between Objectives | Remarks |
|---|---|---|---|
| | | | |
| | | | |
| | | | |
| | | | |
| | | | |
| | | | |
| | | | |
| | | | |
| | | | |
| | | | |
| | | | |
| | | | |
| | | | |
| | | | |
| | | | |
| | | | |
| | | | |
| | | | |
| | | | |

# CRUISING LOG

| Time | Place Abeam: Buoy, Landmark or Other | Distance off | COURSE TO NEXT OBJECTIVE | | | Motor R.P.M. |
|---|---|---|---|---|---|---|
| | | | Course Steered | Magnetic | Distance | |
| | | | | | | |
| | | | | | | |
| | | | | | | |
| | | | | | | |
| | | | | | | |
| | | | | | | |
| | | | | | | |
| | | | | | | |
| | | | | | | |
| | | | | | | |
| | | | | | | |
| | | | | | | |
| | | | | | | |
| | | | | | | |
| | | | | | | |
| | | | | | | |
| | | | | | | |
| | | | | | | |
| | | | | | | |

# CRUISING LOG

| Estimated Speed | Estimated Time to Next Objective | Actual Time Between Objectives | Remarks |
|---|---|---|---|
| | | | |
| | | | |
| | | | |
| | | | |
| | | | |
| | | | |
| | | | |
| | | | |
| | | | |
| | | | |
| | | | |
| | | | |
| | | | |
| | | | |
| | | | |
| | | | |
| | | | |
| | | | |
| | | | |

# CRUISING LOG

| Time | Place Abeam: Buoy, Landmark or Other | Distance off | COURSE TO NEXT OBJECTIVE | | | Motor R.P.M. |
|---|---|---|---|---|---|---|
| | | | Course Steered | Magnetic | Distance | |
| | | | | | | |
| | | | | | | |
| | | | | | | |
| | | | | | | |
| | | | | | | |
| | | | | | | |
| | | | | | | |
| | | | | | | |
| | | | | | | |
| | | | | | | |
| | | | | | | |
| | | | | | | |
| | | | | | | |
| | | | | | | |
| | | | | | | |
| | | | | | | |
| | | | | | | |
| | | | | | | |
| | | | | | | |

# CRUISING LOG

| Estimated Speed | Estimated Time to Next Objective | Actual Time Between Objectives | Remarks |
|---|---|---|---|
| | | | |
| | | | |
| | | | |
| | | | |
| | | | |
| | | | |
| | | | |
| | | | |
| | | | |
| | | | |
| | | | |
| | | | |
| | | | |
| | | | |
| | | | |
| | | | |
| | | | |
| | | | |
| | | | |

# CRUISING LOG

| Time | Place Abeam: Buoy, Landmark or Other | Distance off | COURSE TO NEXT OBJECTIVE | | | Motor R.P.M. |
|---|---|---|---|---|---|---|
| | | | Course Steered | Magnetic | Distance | |
| | | | | | | |
| | | | | | | |
| | | | | | | |
| | | | | | | |
| | | | | | | |
| | | | | | | |
| | | | | | | |
| | | | | | | |
| | | | | | | |
| | | | | | | |
| | | | | | | |
| | | | | | | |
| | | | | | | |
| | | | | | | |
| | | | | | | |
| | | | | | | |
| | | | | | | |
| | | | | | | |
| | | | | | | |

# CRUISING LOG

| Estimated Speed | Estimated Time to Next Objective | Actual Time Between Objectives | Remarks |
|---|---|---|---|
| | | | |
| | | | |
| | | | |
| | | | |
| | | | |
| | | | |
| | | | |
| | | | |
| | | | |
| | | | |
| | | | |
| | | | |
| | | | |
| | | | |
| | | | |
| | | | |
| | | | |
| | | | |
| | | | |

# CRUISING LOG

| Time | Place Abeam: Buoy, Landmark or Other | Distance off | COURSE TO NEXT OBJECTIVE | | | Motor R.P.M. |
|---|---|---|---|---|---|---|
| | | | Course Steered | Magnetic | Distance | |
| | | | | | | |
| | | | | | | |
| | | | | | | |
| | | | | | | |
| | | | | | | |
| | | | | | | |
| | | | | | | |
| | | | | | | |
| | | | | | | |
| | | | | | | |
| | | | | | | |
| | | | | | | |
| | | | | | | |
| | | | | | | |
| | | | | | | |
| | | | | | | |
| | | | | | | |
| | | | | | | |
| | | | | | | |

# CRUISING LOG

| Estimated Speed | Estimated Time to Next Objective | Actual Time Between Objectives | Remarks |
|---|---|---|---|
| | | | |
| | | | |
| | | | |
| | | | |
| | | | |
| | | | |
| | | | |
| | | | |
| | | | |
| | | | |
| | | | |
| | | | |
| | | | |
| | | | |
| | | | |
| | | | |
| | | | |
| | | | |
| | | | |

# CRUISING LOG

| Time | Place Abeam: Buoy, Landmark or Other | Distance off | COURSE TO NEXT OBJECTIVE | | | Motor R.P.M. |
|---|---|---|---|---|---|---|
| | | | Course Steered | Magnetic | Distance | |
| | | | | | | |
| | | | | | | |
| | | | | | | |
| | | | | | | |
| | | | | | | |
| | | | | | | |
| | | | | | | |
| | | | | | | |
| | | | | | | |
| | | | | | | |
| | | | | | | |
| | | | | | | |
| | | | | | | |
| | | | | | | |
| | | | | | | |
| | | | | | | |
| | | | | | | |
| | | | | | | |
| | | | | | | |

# CRUISING LOG

| Estimated Speed | Estimated Time to Next Objective | Actual Time Between Objectives | Remarks |
|---|---|---|---|
| | | | |
| | | | |
| | | | |
| | | | |
| | | | |
| | | | |
| | | | |
| | | | |
| | | | |
| | | | |
| | | | |
| | | | |
| | | | |
| | | | |
| | | | |
| | | | |
| | | | |
| | | | |
| | | | |

# CRUISING LOG

| Time | Place Abeam: Buoy, Landmark or Other | Distance off | COURSE TO NEXT OBJECTIVE | | | Motor R.P.M. |
|---|---|---|---|---|---|---|
| | | | Course Steered | Magnetic | Distance | |
| | | | | | | |
| | | | | | | |
| | | | | | | |
| | | | | | | |
| | | | | | | |
| | | | | | | |
| | | | | | | |
| | | | | | | |
| | | | | | | |
| | | | | | | |
| | | | | | | |
| | | | | | | |
| | | | | | | |
| | | | | | | |
| | | | | | | |
| | | | | | | |
| | | | | | | |
| | | | | | | |
| | | | | | | |

# CRUISING LOG

| Estimated Speed | Estimated Time to Next Objective | Actual Time Between Objectives | Remarks |
|---|---|---|---|
| | | | |
| | | | |
| | | | |
| | | | |
| | | | |
| | | | |
| | | | |
| | | | |
| | | | |
| | | | |
| | | | |
| | | | |
| | | | |
| | | | |
| | | | |
| | | | |
| | | | |
| | | | |
| | | | |

# CRUISING LOG

| Time | Place Abeam: Buoy, Landmark or Other | Distance off | COURSE TO NEXT OBJECTIVE | | | Motor R.P.M. |
|---|---|---|---|---|---|---|
| | | | Course Steered | Magnetic | Distance | |
| | | | | | | |
| | | | | | | |
| | | | | | | |
| | | | | | | |
| | | | | | | |
| | | | | | | |
| | | | | | | |
| | | | | | | |
| | | | | | | |
| | | | | | | |
| | | | | | | |
| | | | | | | |
| | | | | | | |
| | | | | | | |
| | | | | | | |
| | | | | | | |
| | | | | | | |
| | | | | | | |

# CRUISING LOG

| Estimated Speed | Estimated Time to Next Objective | Actual Time Between Objectives | Remarks |
|---|---|---|---|
| | | | |
| | | | |
| | | | |
| | | | |
| | | | |
| | | | |
| | | | |
| | | | |
| | | | |
| | | | |
| | | | |
| | | | |
| | | | |
| | | | |
| | | | |
| | | | |
| | | | |
| | | | |
| | | | |

# CRUISING LOG

| Time | Place Abeam: Buoy, Landmark or Other | Distance off | COURSE TO NEXT OBJECTIVE | | | Motor R.P.M. |
|---|---|---|---|---|---|---|
| | | | Course Steered | Magnetic | Distance | |
| | | | | | | |
| | | | | | | |
| | | | | | | |
| | | | | | | |
| | | | | | | |
| | | | | | | |
| | | | | | | |
| | | | | | | |
| | | | | | | |
| | | | | | | |
| | | | | | | |
| | | | | | | |
| | | | | | | |
| | | | | | | |
| | | | | | | |
| | | | | | | |
| | | | | | | |
| | | | | | | |
| | | | | | | |

# CRUISING LOG

| Estimated Speed | Estimated Time to Next Objective | Actual Time Between Objectives | Remarks |
|---|---|---|---|
| | | | |
| | | | |
| | | | |
| | | | |
| | | | |
| | | | |
| | | | |
| | | | |
| | | | |
| | | | |
| | | | |
| | | | |
| | | | |
| | | | |
| | | | |
| | | | |
| | | | |
| | | | |
| | | | |

# CRUISING LOG

| Time | Place Abeam: Buoy, Landmark or Other | Distance off | COURSE TO NEXT OBJECTIVE | | | Motor R.P.M. |
|---|---|---|---|---|---|---|
| | | | Course Steered | Magnetic | Distance | |
| | | | | | | |
| | | | | | | |
| | | | | | | |
| | | | | | | |
| | | | | | | |
| | | | | | | |
| | | | | | | |
| | | | | | | |
| | | | | | | |
| | | | | | | |
| | | | | | | |
| | | | | | | |
| | | | | | | |
| | | | | | | |
| | | | | | | |
| | | | | | | |
| | | | | | | |
| | | | | | | |
| | | | | | | |

# CRUISING LOG

| Estimated Speed | Estimated Time to Next Objective | Actual Time Between Objectives | Remarks |
|---|---|---|---|
| | | | |
| | | | |
| | | | |
| | | | |
| | | | |
| | | | |
| | | | |
| | | | |
| | | | |
| | | | |
| | | | |
| | | | |
| | | | |
| | | | |
| | | | |
| | | | |
| | | | |
| | | | |
| | | | |

# CRUISING LOG

| Time | Place Abeam: Buoy, Landmark or Other | Distance off | COURSE TO NEXT OBJECTIVE | | | Motor R.P.M. |
|---|---|---|---|---|---|---|
| | | | Course Steered | Magnetic | Distance | |
| | | | | | | |
| | | | | | | |
| | | | | | | |
| | | | | | | |
| | | | | | | |
| | | | | | | |
| | | | | | | |
| | | | | | | |
| | | | | | | |
| | | | | | | |
| | | | | | | |
| | | | | | | |
| | | | | | | |
| | | | | | | |
| | | | | | | |
| | | | | | | |
| | | | | | | |
| | | | | | | |
| | | | | | | |

# CRUISING LOG

| Estimated Speed | Estimated Time to Next Objective | Actual Time Between Objectives | Remarks |
|---|---|---|---|
| | | | |
| | | | |
| | | | |
| | | | |
| | | | |
| | | | |
| | | | |
| | | | |
| | | | |
| | | | |
| | | | |
| | | | |
| | | | |
| | | | |
| | | | |
| | | | |
| | | | |
| | | | |
| | | | |

# CRUISING LOG

| Time | Place Abeam: Buoy, Landmark or Other | Distance off | COURSE TO NEXT OBJECTIVE | | | Motor R.P.M. |
|---|---|---|---|---|---|---|
| | | | Course Steered | Magnetic | Distance | |
| | | | | | | |
| | | | | | | |
| | | | | | | |
| | | | | | | |
| | | | | | | |
| | | | | | | |
| | | | | | | |
| | | | | | | |
| | | | | | | |
| | | | | | | |
| | | | | | | |
| | | | | | | |
| | | | | | | |
| | | | | | | |
| | | | | | | |
| | | | | | | |
| | | | | | | |
| | | | | | | |
| | | | | | | |

# CRUISING LOG

| Estimated Speed | Estimated Time to Next Objective | Actual Time Between Objectives | Remarks |
|---|---|---|---|
| | | | |
| | | | |
| | | | |
| | | | |
| | | | |
| | | | |
| | | | |
| | | | |
| | | | |
| | | | |
| | | | |
| | | | |
| | | | |
| | | | |
| | | | |
| | | | |
| | | | |
| | | | |
| | | | |

# CRUISING LOG

| Time | Place Abeam: Buoy, Landmark or Other | Distance off | COURSE TO NEXT OBJECTIVE | | | Motor R.P.M. |
|---|---|---|---|---|---|---|
| | | | Course Steered | Magnetic | Distance | |
| | | | | | | |
| | | | | | | |
| | | | | | | |
| | | | | | | |
| | | | | | | |
| | | | | | | |
| | | | | | | |
| | | | | | | |
| | | | | | | |
| | | | | | | |
| | | | | | | |
| | | | | | | |
| | | | | | | |
| | | | | | | |
| | | | | | | |
| | | | | | | |
| | | | | | | |
| | | | | | | |
| | | | | | | |

# CRUISING LOG

| Estimated Speed | Estimated Time to Next Objective | Actual Time Between Objectives | Remarks |
|---|---|---|---|
| | | | |
| | | | |
| | | | |
| | | | |
| | | | |
| | | | |
| | | | |
| | | | |
| | | | |
| | | | |
| | | | |
| | | | |
| | | | |
| | | | |
| | | | |
| | | | |
| | | | |
| | | | |
| | | | |

# CRUISING LOG

| Time | Place Abeam: Buoy, Landmark or Other | Distance off | COURSE TO NEXT OBJECTIVE | | | Motor R.P.M. |
|---|---|---|---|---|---|---|
| | | | Course Steered | Magnetic | Distance | |
| | | | | | | |
| | | | | | | |
| | | | | | | |
| | | | | | | |
| | | | | | | |
| | | | | | | |
| | | | | | | |
| | | | | | | |
| | | | | | | |
| | | | | | | |
| | | | | | | |
| | | | | | | |
| | | | | | | |
| | | | | | | |
| | | | | | | |
| | | | | | | |
| | | | | | | |
| | | | | | | |
| | | | | | | |

# CRUISING LOG

| Estimated Speed | Estimated Time to Next Objective | Actual Time Between Objectives | Remarks |
|---|---|---|---|
| | | | |
| | | | |
| | | | |
| | | | |
| | | | |
| | | | |
| | | | |
| | | | |
| | | | |
| | | | |
| | | | |
| | | | |
| | | | |
| | | | |
| | | | |
| | | | |
| | | | |
| | | | |
| | | | |

# CRUISING LOG

| Time | Place Abeam: Buoy, Landmark or Other | Distance off | COURSE TO NEXT OBJECTIVE | | | Motor R.P.M. |
|---|---|---|---|---|---|---|
| | | | Course Steered | Magnetic | Distance | |
| | | | | | | |
| | | | | | | |
| | | | | | | |
| | | | | | | |
| | | | | | | |
| | | | | | | |
| | | | | | | |
| | | | | | | |
| | | | | | | |
| | | | | | | |
| | | | | | | |
| | | | | | | |
| | | | | | | |
| | | | | | | |
| | | | | | | |
| | | | | | | |
| | | | | | | |
| | | | | | | |
| | | | | | | |

# CRUISING LOG

| Estimated Speed | Estimated Time to Next Objective | Actual Time Between Objectives | Remarks |
|---|---|---|---|
| | | | |
| | | | |
| | | | |
| | | | |
| | | | |
| | | | |
| | | | |
| | | | |
| | | | |
| | | | |
| | | | |
| | | | |
| | | | |
| | | | |
| | | | |
| | | | |
| | | | |
| | | | |
| | | | |

# CRUISING LOG

| Time | Place Abeam: Buoy, Landmark or Other | Distance off | COURSE TO NEXT OBJECTIVE | | | Motor R.P.M. |
|---|---|---|---|---|---|---|
| | | | Course Steered | Magnetic | Distance | |
| | | | | | | |
| | | | | | | |
| | | | | | | |
| | | | | | | |
| | | | | | | |
| | | | | | | |
| | | | | | | |
| | | | | | | |
| | | | | | | |
| | | | | | | |
| | | | | | | |
| | | | | | | |
| | | | | | | |
| | | | | | | |
| | | | | | | |
| | | | | | | |
| | | | | | | |
| | | | | | | |
| | | | | | | |

# CRUISING LOG

| Estimated Speed | Estimated Time to Next Objective | Actual Time Between Objectives | Remarks |
|---|---|---|---|
| | | | |
| | | | |
| | | | |
| | | | |
| | | | |
| | | | |
| | | | |
| | | | |
| | | | |
| | | | |
| | | | |
| | | | |
| | | | |
| | | | |
| | | | |
| | | | |
| | | | |
| | | | |
| | | | |

# CRUISING LOG

| Time | Place Abeam: Buoy, Landmark or Other | Distance off | COURSE TO NEXT OBJECTIVE | | | Motor R.P.M. |
|---|---|---|---|---|---|---|
| | | | Course Steered | Magnetic | Distance | |
| | | | | | | |
| | | | | | | |
| | | | | | | |
| | | | | | | |
| | | | | | | |
| | | | | | | |
| | | | | | | |
| | | | | | | |
| | | | | | | |
| | | | | | | |
| | | | | | | |
| | | | | | | |
| | | | | | | |
| | | | | | | |
| | | | | | | |
| | | | | | | |
| | | | | | | |
| | | | | | | |
| | | | | | | |

# CRUISING LOG

| Estimated Speed | Estimated Time to Next Objective | Actual Time Between Objectives | Remarks |
|---|---|---|---|
| | | | |
| | | | |
| | | | |
| | | | |
| | | | |
| | | | |
| | | | |
| | | | |
| | | | |
| | | | |
| | | | |
| | | | |
| | | | |
| | | | |
| | | | |
| | | | |
| | | | |
| | | | |
| | | | |

# CRUISING LOG

| Time | Place Abeam: Buoy, Landmark or Other | Distance off | COURSE TO NEXT OBJECTIVE | | | Motor R.P.M. |
|---|---|---|---|---|---|---|
| | | | Course Steered | Magnetic | Distance | |
| | | | | | | |
| | | | | | | |
| | | | | | | |
| | | | | | | |
| | | | | | | |
| | | | | | | |
| | | | | | | |
| | | | | | | |
| | | | | | | |
| | | | | | | |
| | | | | | | |
| | | | | | | |
| | | | | | | |
| | | | | | | |
| | | | | | | |
| | | | | | | |
| | | | | | | |
| | | | | | | |
| | | | | | | |

# CRUISING LOG

| Estimated Speed | Estimated Time to Next Objective | Actual Time Between Objectives | Remarks |
|---|---|---|---|
| | | | |
| | | | |
| | | | |
| | | | |
| | | | |
| | | | |
| | | | |
| | | | |
| | | | |
| | | | |
| | | | |
| | | | |
| | | | |
| | | | |
| | | | |
| | | | |
| | | | |
| | | | |
| | | | |

# CRUISING LOG

| Time | Place Abeam: Buoy, Landmark or Other | Distance off | COURSE TO NEXT OBJECTIVE | | | Motor R.P.M. |
|---|---|---|---|---|---|---|
| | | | Course Steered | Magnetic | Distance | |
| | | | | | | |
| | | | | | | |
| | | | | | | |
| | | | | | | |
| | | | | | | |
| | | | | | | |
| | | | | | | |
| | | | | | | |
| | | | | | | |
| | | | | | | |
| | | | | | | |
| | | | | | | |
| | | | | | | |
| | | | | | | |
| | | | | | | |
| | | | | | | |
| | | | | | | |
| | | | | | | |
| | | | | | | |

# CRUISING LOG

| Estimated Speed | Estimated Time to Next Objective | Actual Time Between Objectives | Remarks |
|---|---|---|---|
| | | | |
| | | | |
| | | | |
| | | | |
| | | | |
| | | | |
| | | | |
| | | | |
| | | | |
| | | | |
| | | | |
| | | | |
| | | | |
| | | | |
| | | | |
| | | | |
| | | | |
| | | | |
| | | | |

# CRUISING LOG

| Time | Place Abeam: Buoy, Landmark or Other | Distance off | COURSE TO NEXT OBJECTIVE | | | Motor R.P.M. |
|---|---|---|---|---|---|---|
| | | | Course Steered | Magnetic | Distance | |
| | | | | | | |
| | | | | | | |
| | | | | | | |
| | | | | | | |
| | | | | | | |
| | | | | | | |
| | | | | | | |
| | | | | | | |
| | | | | | | |
| | | | | | | |
| | | | | | | |
| | | | | | | |
| | | | | | | |
| | | | | | | |
| | | | | | | |
| | | | | | | |
| | | | | | | |
| | | | | | | |

# CRUISING LOG

| Estimated Speed | Estimated Time to Next Objective | Actual Time Between Objectives | Remarks |
|---|---|---|---|
| | | | |
| | | | |
| | | | |
| | | | |
| | | | |
| | | | |
| | | | |
| | | | |
| | | | |
| | | | |
| | | | |
| | | | |
| | | | |
| | | | |
| | | | |
| | | | |
| | | | |
| | | | |
| | | | |

# CRUISING LOG

| Time | Place Abeam: Buoy, Landmark or Other | Distance off | COURSE TO NEXT OBJECTIVE | | | Motor R.P.M. |
|---|---|---|---|---|---|---|
| | | | Course Steered | Magnetic | Distance | |
| | | | | | | |
| | | | | | | |
| | | | | | | |
| | | | | | | |
| | | | | | | |
| | | | | | | |
| | | | | | | |
| | | | | | | |
| | | | | | | |
| | | | | | | |
| | | | | | | |
| | | | | | | |
| | | | | | | |
| | | | | | | |
| | | | | | | |
| | | | | | | |
| | | | | | | |
| | | | | | | |
| | | | | | | |

# CRUISING LOG

| Estimated Speed | Estimated Time to Next Objective | Actual Time Between Objectives | Remarks |
|---|---|---|---|
| | | | |
| | | | |
| | | | |
| | | | |
| | | | |
| | | | |
| | | | |
| | | | |
| | | | |
| | | | |
| | | | |
| | | | |
| | | | |
| | | | |
| | | | |
| | | | |
| | | | |
| | | | |
| | | | |

# CRUISING LOG

| Time | Place Abeam: Buoy, Landmark or Other | Distance off | COURSE TO NEXT OBJECTIVE | | | Motor R.P.M. |
|---|---|---|---|---|---|---|
| | | | Course Steered | Magnetic | Distance | |
| | | | | | | |
| | | | | | | |
| | | | | | | |
| | | | | | | |
| | | | | | | |
| | | | | | | |
| | | | | | | |
| | | | | | | |
| | | | | | | |
| | | | | | | |
| | | | | | | |
| | | | | | | |
| | | | | | | |
| | | | | | | |
| | | | | | | |
| | | | | | | |
| | | | | | | |
| | | | | | | |
| | | | | | | |

# CRUISING LOG

| Estimated Speed | Estimated Time to Next Objective | Actual Time Between Objectives | Remarks |
|---|---|---|---|
| | | | |
| | | | |
| | | | |
| | | | |
| | | | |
| | | | |
| | | | |
| | | | |
| | | | |
| | | | |
| | | | |
| | | | |
| | | | |
| | | | |
| | | | |
| | | | |
| | | | |
| | | | |
| | | | |

# CRUISING LOG

| Time | Place Abeam: Buoy, Landmark or Other | Distance off | COURSE TO NEXT OBJECTIVE | | | Motor R.P.M. |
|---|---|---|---|---|---|---|
| | | | Course Steered | Magnetic | Distance | |
| | | | | | | |
| | | | | | | |
| | | | | | | |
| | | | | | | |
| | | | | | | |
| | | | | | | |
| | | | | | | |
| | | | | | | |
| | | | | | | |
| | | | | | | |
| | | | | | | |
| | | | | | | |
| | | | | | | |
| | | | | | | |
| | | | | | | |
| | | | | | | |
| | | | | | | |
| | | | | | | |
| | | | | | | |

# CRUISING LOG

| Estimated Speed | Estimated Time to Next Objective | Actual Time Between Objectives | Remarks |
|---|---|---|---|
| | | | |
| | | | |
| | | | |
| | | | |
| | | | |
| | | | |
| | | | |
| | | | |
| | | | |
| | | | |
| | | | |
| | | | |
| | | | |
| | | | |
| | | | |
| | | | |
| | | | |
| | | | |
| | | | |

# CRUISING LOG

| Time | Place Abeam: Buoy, Landmark or Other | Distance off | COURSE TO NEXT OBJECTIVE | | | Motor R.P.M. |
|---|---|---|---|---|---|---|
| | | | Course Steered | Magnetic | Distance | |
| | | | | | | |
| | | | | | | |
| | | | | | | |
| | | | | | | |
| | | | | | | |
| | | | | | | |
| | | | | | | |
| | | | | | | |
| | | | | | | |
| | | | | | | |
| | | | | | | |
| | | | | | | |
| | | | | | | |
| | | | | | | |
| | | | | | | |
| | | | | | | |
| | | | | | | |
| | | | | | | |
| | | | | | | |

# CRUISING LOG

| Estimated Speed | Estimated Time to Next Objective | Actual Time Between Objectives | Remarks |
|---|---|---|---|
| | | | |
| | | | |
| | | | |
| | | | |
| | | | |
| | | | |
| | | | |
| | | | |
| | | | |
| | | | |
| | | | |
| | | | |
| | | | |
| | | | |
| | | | |
| | | | |
| | | | |
| | | | |
| | | | |

# CRUISING LOG

| Time | Place Abeam: Buoy, Landmark or Other | Distance off | COURSE TO NEXT OBJECTIVE | | | Motor R.P.M. |
|---|---|---|---|---|---|---|
| | | | Course Steered | Magnetic | Distance | |
| | | | | | | |
| | | | | | | |
| | | | | | | |
| | | | | | | |
| | | | | | | |
| | | | | | | |
| | | | | | | |
| | | | | | | |
| | | | | | | |
| | | | | | | |
| | | | | | | |
| | | | | | | |
| | | | | | | |
| | | | | | | |
| | | | | | | |
| | | | | | | |
| | | | | | | |
| | | | | | | |
| | | | | | | |

# CRUISING LOG

| Estimated Speed | Estimated Time to Next Objective | Actual Time Between Objectives | Remarks |
|---|---|---|---|
| | | | |
| | | | |
| | | | |
| | | | |
| | | | |
| | | | |
| | | | |
| | | | |
| | | | |
| | | | |
| | | | |
| | | | |
| | | | |
| | | | |
| | | | |
| | | | |
| | | | |
| | | | |
| | | | |

# CRUISING LOG

| Time | Place Abeam: Buoy, Landmark or Other | Distance off | COURSE TO NEXT OBJECTIVE | | | Motor R.P.M. |
|---|---|---|---|---|---|---|
| | | | Course Steered | Magnetic | Distance | |
| | | | | | | |
| | | | | | | |
| | | | | | | |
| | | | | | | |
| | | | | | | |
| | | | | | | |
| | | | | | | |
| | | | | | | |
| | | | | | | |
| | | | | | | |
| | | | | | | |
| | | | | | | |
| | | | | | | |
| | | | | | | |
| | | | | | | |
| | | | | | | |
| | | | | | | |
| | | | | | | |
| | | | | | | |

# CRUISING LOG

| Estimated Speed | Estimated Time to Next Objective | Actual Time Between Objectives | Remarks |
|---|---|---|---|
| | | | |
| | | | |
| | | | |
| | | | |
| | | | |
| | | | |
| | | | |
| | | | |
| | | | |
| | | | |
| | | | |
| | | | |
| | | | |
| | | | |
| | | | |
| | | | |
| | | | |
| | | | |
| | | | |

# CRUISING LOG

| Time | Place Abeam: Buoy, Landmark or Other | Distance off | COURSE TO NEXT OBJECTIVE | | | Motor R.P.M. |
|---|---|---|---|---|---|---|
| | | | Course Steered | Magnetic | Distance | |
| | | | | | | |
| | | | | | | |
| | | | | | | |
| | | | | | | |
| | | | | | | |
| | | | | | | |
| | | | | | | |
| | | | | | | |
| | | | | | | |
| | | | | | | |
| | | | | | | |
| | | | | | | |
| | | | | | | |
| | | | | | | |
| | | | | | | |
| | | | | | | |
| | | | | | | |
| | | | | | | |
| | | | | | | |

# CRUISING LOG

| Estimated Speed | Estimated Time to Next Objective | Actual Time Between Objectives | Remarks |
|---|---|---|---|
| | | | |
| | | | |
| | | | |
| | | | |
| | | | |
| | | | |
| | | | |
| | | | |
| | | | |
| | | | |
| | | | |
| | | | |
| | | | |
| | | | |
| | | | |
| | | | |
| | | | |
| | | | |
| | | | |

# CRUISING LOG

| Time | Place Abeam: Buoy, Landmark or Other | Distance off | COURSE TO NEXT OBJECTIVE | | | Motor R.P.M. |
|---|---|---|---|---|---|---|
| | | | Course Steered | Magnetic | Distance | |
| | | | | | | |
| | | | | | | |
| | | | | | | |
| | | | | | | |
| | | | | | | |
| | | | | | | |
| | | | | | | |
| | | | | | | |
| | | | | | | |
| | | | | | | |
| | | | | | | |
| | | | | | | |
| | | | | | | |
| | | | | | | |
| | | | | | | |
| | | | | | | |
| | | | | | | |
| | | | | | | |
| | | | | | | |

# CRUISING LOG

| Estimated Speed | Estimated Time to Next Objective | Actual Time Between Objectives | Remarks |
|---|---|---|---|
| | | | |
| | | | |
| | | | |
| | | | |
| | | | |
| | | | |
| | | | |
| | | | |
| | | | |
| | | | |
| | | | |
| | | | |
| | | | |
| | | | |
| | | | |
| | | | |
| | | | |
| | | | |
| | | | |

# CRUISING LOG

| Time | Place Abeam: Buoy, Landmark or Other | Distance off | COURSE TO NEXT OBJECTIVE | | | Motor R.P.M. |
|---|---|---|---|---|---|---|
| | | | Course Steered | Magnetic | Distance | |
| | | | | | | |
| | | | | | | |
| | | | | | | |
| | | | | | | |
| | | | | | | |
| | | | | | | |
| | | | | | | |
| | | | | | | |
| | | | | | | |
| | | | | | | |
| | | | | | | |
| | | | | | | |
| | | | | | | |
| | | | | | | |
| | | | | | | |
| | | | | | | |
| | | | | | | |
| | | | | | | |

# CRUISING LOG

| Estimated Speed | Estimated Time to Next Objective | Actual Time Between Objectives | Remarks |
|---|---|---|---|
| | | | |
| | | | |
| | | | |
| | | | |
| | | | |
| | | | |
| | | | |
| | | | |
| | | | |
| | | | |
| | | | |
| | | | |
| | | | |
| | | | |
| | | | |
| | | | |
| | | | |
| | | | |
| | | | |

# RADIO/TELEPHONE LOG

| Date | Time | Yacht or Station Called | Call Letters or Telephone Number | Location of Called Number | Name of Operator |
|---|---|---|---|---|---|
| | | | | | |
| | | | | | |
| | | | | | |
| | | | | | |
| | | | | | |
| | | | | | |
| | | | | | |
| | | | | | |
| | | | | | |
| | | | | | |
| | | | | | |
| | | | | | |
| | | | | | |
| | | | | | |
| | | | | | |
| | | | | | |
| | | | | | |
| | | | | | |
| | | | | | |
| | | | | | |
| | | | | | |

# RADIO/TELEPHONE LOG

| Date | Time | Yacht or Station Called | Call Letters or Telephone Number | Location of Called Number | Name of Operator |
|---|---|---|---|---|---|
| | | | | | |
| | | | | | |
| | | | | | |
| | | | | | |
| | | | | | |
| | | | | | |
| | | | | | |
| | | | | | |
| | | | | | |
| | | | | | |
| | | | | | |
| | | | | | |
| | | | | | |
| | | | | | |
| | | | | | |
| | | | | | |
| | | | | | |
| | | | | | |
| | | | | | |
| | | | | | |
| | | | | | |

# RADIO/TELEPHONE LOG

| Date | Time | Yacht or Station Called | Call Letters or Telephone Number | Location of Called Number | Name of Operator |
|---|---|---|---|---|---|
| | | | | | |
| | | | | | |
| | | | | | |
| | | | | | |
| | | | | | |
| | | | | | |
| | | | | | |
| | | | | | |
| | | | | | |
| | | | | | |
| | | | | | |
| | | | | | |
| | | | | | |
| | | | | | |
| | | | | | |
| | | | | | |
| | | | | | |
| | | | | | |
| | | | | | |
| | | | | | |
| | | | | | |

# RADIO/TELEPHONE LOG

| Date | Time | Yacht or Station Called | Call Letters or Telephone Number | Location of Called Number | Name of Operator |
|---|---|---|---|---|---|
| | | | | | |
| | | | | | |
| | | | | | |
| | | | | | |
| | | | | | |
| | | | | | |
| | | | | | |
| | | | | | |
| | | | | | |
| | | | | | |
| | | | | | |
| | | | | | |
| | | | | | |
| | | | | | |
| | | | | | |
| | | | | | |
| | | | | | |
| | | | | | |
| | | | | | |
| | | | | | |
| | | | | | |

# RADIO/TELEPHONE LOG

| Date | Time | Yacht or Station Called | Call Letters or Telephone Number | Location of Called Number | Name of Operator |
|---|---|---|---|---|---|
| | | | | | |
| | | | | | |
| | | | | | |
| | | | | | |
| | | | | | |
| | | | | | |
| | | | | | |
| | | | | | |
| | | | | | |
| | | | | | |
| | | | | | |
| | | | | | |
| | | | | | |
| | | | | | |
| | | | | | |
| | | | | | |
| | | | | | |
| | | | | | |
| | | | | | |
| | | | | | |
| | | | | | |

# RADIO/TELEPHONE LOG

| Date | Time | Yacht or Station Called | Call Letters or Telephone Number | Location of Called Number | Name of Operator |
|---|---|---|---|---|---|
| | | | | | |
| | | | | | |
| | | | | | |
| | | | | | |
| | | | | | |
| | | | | | |
| | | | | | |
| | | | | | |
| | | | | | |
| | | | | | |
| | | | | | |
| | | | | | |
| | | | | | |
| | | | | | |
| | | | | | |
| | | | | | |
| | | | | | |
| | | | | | |
| | | | | | |
| | | | | | |
| | | | | | |

# RADIO/TELEPHONE LOG

| Date | Time | Yacht or Station Called | Call Letters or Telephone Number | Location of Called Number | Name of Operator |
|---|---|---|---|---|---|
| | | | | | |
| | | | | | |
| | | | | | |
| | | | | | |
| | | | | | |
| | | | | | |
| | | | | | |
| | | | | | |
| | | | | | |
| | | | | | |
| | | | | | |
| | | | | | |
| | | | | | |
| | | | | | |
| | | | | | |
| | | | | | |
| | | | | | |
| | | | | | |
| | | | | | |
| | | | | | |
| | | | | | |

# RADIO/TELEPHONE LOG

| Date | Time | Yacht or Station Called | Call Letters or Telephone Number | Location of Called Number | Name of Operator |
|---|---|---|---|---|---|
| | | | | | |
| | | | | | |
| | | | | | |
| | | | | | |
| | | | | | |
| | | | | | |
| | | | | | |
| | | | | | |
| | | | | | |
| | | | | | |
| | | | | | |
| | | | | | |
| | | | | | |
| | | | | | |
| | | | | | |
| | | | | | |
| | | | | | |
| | | | | | |
| | | | | | |
| | | | | | |
| | | | | | |

# CRUISING RECIPES

**Write In Space For Cruising Recipes**

# CRUISING RECIPES

**Let Friends Autograph Favorite Recipes**

# CHILDREN'S LOG

**These Pages Are for Messages and Autographs**

# CHILDREN'S LOG

**Snapshots**

**Children's Drawings**

# WEATHER SYMBOLS FOR A LOG

As a convenience in recording weather information, a standard code has been developed which includes the famous Beaufort Scale—the identification of wind strength by a number.

*General Weather: b*—clear blue sky; *d*—drizzle or light rain; *f*—fog or foggy; *g*—gloomy or stormy-looking; *h*—hail; *l*—lightning; *m*—misty; *p*—passing shower; *q*—squally; *r*—rain; *s*—snow; *t*—thunder; *u*—ugly appearance or threatening; *w*—wet or heavy dew; *z*—hazy.

*Sea State: B*—broken or irregular; *C*—choppy, short or cross sea; *G*—ground swell; *H*—heavy sea; *L*—long rolling sea; *M*—moderate sea or swell; *R*—rough; *S*—smooth; *T*—tide rips.

*Wind Force: 0*—calm; *1*—light air; *2*—light breeze; *3*—gentle breeze; *4*—moderate breeze; *5*—fresh breeze; *6*—strong breeze; *7*—moderate gale; *8*—fresh gale; *9*—strong gale; *10*—whole gale; *11*—storm; *12*—hurricane.

*Cloud forms: Ci*—Cirrus; *Ci-S*—Cirro-Stratus; *Ci-Cu*—Cirro-Cumulus; *A-Cu*—Alto-Cumulus; *A-S*—Alto-Stratus; *S-Cu*—Strato-Cumulus; *N*—Nimbus; *Cu*—Cumulus; *Cu-N*—Cumulo-Nimbus; *S*—Stratus; *Fr-Cu*—Fracto-Cumulus; *Fr-S*—Fracto-Stratus.

*Cloud Cover:* In the scale for the amount of clouds, 0 represents a cloudless sky and 10 a sky which is completely overcast.

# SHIP'S PAPERS/LICENSING

If you are a new boat owner, or are moving from one state to another, the following information on licensing and on the Coast Guard will be helpful.

The technical term for boat licensing is "numbering," in some cases. Following is a brief look at the relationship between federal and state laws, as well as the various addresses where information may be obtained.

## State Boating Laws

Federal laws and regulations now preempt State controls in the area of boat and equipment safety standards, but the Federal Boat Safety Act of 1971 does allow States to impose requirements for safety equipment beyond Federal rules if needed to meet uniquely hazardous local circumstances. The Act does not preempt State or local laws and regulations directed at safe boat operation. In addition, there are usually laws and regulations relating to boat trailers and their use.

The old saying that "Ignorance of the law is no excuse" is quite applicable to skippers of recreational boats. Each should know the requirements and restrictions of his state, and should take steps as appropriate to expand his knowledge if he plans to cruise in other states. He should particularly be alert to varying state laws about boat trailering on highways.

Information on applicable state laws and regulations may be obtained from each state, usually from the same office that handles registration and numbering. The Outboard Boating Club of America publishes four regional handbooks that are thorough compilations of laws and regulations relating to boats of all sizes, trailers, boating activities, and taxation. These are up-dated when necessary by supplements. These may be ordered from OBC at 401 N. Michigan Avenue, Chicago, Illinois 60611.

Not all boats are numbered—many are "documented." This is a process whereby official papers on the craft are issued by the Coast Guard in much the same manner as for large ships. (Formerly this was done by the Bureau of Customs of the Treasury Department, but the function was transferred to the Coast Guard in 1966.) The numbering requirements of the 1971 Federal Boat Safety Act do not apply to documented vessels; other provisions of this Act, however, do apply to "boats" as defined therein.

## Documentation

Documentation of a craft used solely for non-commercial recreational purposes is optional, and certain requirements must be met. The vessel must be owned by a citizen of the United States (or a corporation 51% or more owned by U.S. citizens) and it must be of a specified minimum size, 5 tons as explained below. The captain of a documented vessel, if other than the owner, must be a U.S. citizen.

Before a vessel can be documented it must be measured for its tonnage. ("Admeasured" is the more formal term, but it means the same and is gradually being dropped in favor of the simpler language.)

## Types of Documents

The documents that are issued to vessels are of five forms—register, enrollment and license, license, yacht enrollment and license, and yacht license. Only the latter two are of interest to the owners of noncommercial craft, but all should be generally understood.

A yacht enrollment and license may be issued to a vessel of 20 net tons or more used exclusively for pleasure. A yacht license may be issued to such a vessel of 5 net tons or over but less than 20 net tons.

Important privileges extended by documentation of vessels as yachts include (1) legal authority to fly the yacht ensign, which authority is not formally granted to other boats; and (2) the privilege of recording bills of sale, mortgages, and other instruments of title for the vessel with federal officials at her home port, giving constructive legal notice to all persons of the effect of such instruments and permitting the attainment of a preferred status for mortgages so recorded. This gives additional security to the purchaser or mortgagee and facilitates financing and transfer of title for such vessels.

A procedure has been established under which the owner of a boat used *exclusively for pleasure* may file an "Application for Simplified Admeasurement" with the Officer in Charge, Marine Inspection in his local Coast Guard District.

## Tonnage

In brief, the simplified measurement method uses the numerical product of three dimensions—the overall length (L), overall breadth (B), and depth (D)—note that this is "depth," an internal dimension, and not the boat's "draft." The gross tonnage of a vessel designed for sailing is assumed to be ½(LBD/100); for vessels not designed for sailing it is calculated to be ⅔(LBD/100).

The gross tonnage of a catamaran or a trimaran is determined by adding the gross tonnages of each hull as calculated above.

Where the volume of the deckhouse is disproportionate to the volume of the hull—as in some designs of houseboats—the volume of the deckhouse, calculated by appropriate geometric formulas and expressed in tons of 100 cubic feet each, is added to the gross tonnage of the hull as calculated with L, B, and D.

The net tonnage of a sailing vessel is recorded as $\frac{9}{10}$ of the gross tonnage; for a non-sailing vessel, the multiplying factor is $\frac{8}{10}$. If there is no propelling machinery in the hull, the net tonnage will be the same as the gross tonnage.

## Obtaining Documentation

Application for simplified admeasurement is by letter; there is no standard form of application unless one has been prepared by the local Officer in Charge, Marine Inspection. The owner may take his own length, breadth, and depth measurements and complete the transaction by mail, quickly and without cost.

Considerable information on documentation can be obtained from the Coast Guard pamphlet "Yacht Admeasurement and Documentation"–CG-177, available without charge from Coast Guard offices.

The owner of a boat may elect to have formal measurement rather than use the simplified method; this is *required* if the vessel is to be used *commercially*.

If an owner is contemplating formal admeasurement, it is suggested that he first make an estimate of the tonnage by using the simplified method. If the resulting net tonnage is less than 5 tons, it is not likely that the vessel will be 5 net tons or more when formally measured.

## Formal Measurement

An application for formal measurement should be prepared in writing and submitted to the Officer in Charge, Marine Inspection, for the area in which the vessel is located. The information that must be submitted is listed in CG-177.

Under formal measurement procedures, a definite date and place should be agreed upon between the measuring officer and the owner, or his agent, so that the vessel may be physically measured and examined.

The measuring officer who calculates the tonnages by the simplified method, or who visits the vessel for formal measurement, will provide the necessary forms which must be filled out to receive the document. Further assistance may be obtained by writing, called, or visiting the nearest Documentation Office, U.S. Coast Guard.

A vessel may be documented only in the name of the holder of legal title. It is necessary therefore for the owner to present adequate title papers with his application.

## Establishing Title

If the vessel was built for the present owner and has never been owned by anyone else, that person should have the builder furnish a "Builder's Certificate" on Form 1261 to establish title.

## SHIP'S PAPERS/LICENSING

If there were previous owners, the proper documents are the Builder's Certificate and bills of sale in recordable form from each of the previous owners, preferably on Form 1346, available without charge from the Documentation Office. If these steps are impracticable, consult the Officer in Charge, Marine Inspection, for alternative procedures.

### Fees

The charge for the documentation of a yacht is $75. Annual renewal is $15. There is no charge for measuring and certifying the tonnages of a vessel, except that if the physical presence of a measuring officer is required outside certain local limits, a charge is made to cover his salary, travel, and subsistence expenses. If a vessel is to be measured on a Saturday or Sunday, substantial charges for overtime may be involved; it is suggested that a convenient weekday be proposed in the application to avoid such charges.

A small charge is made for recording each bill of sale or other recordable title instrument; the average cost of recording a bill of sale is approximately $2.

### Markings of a Documented Boat

The owner or master of a vessel to be documented must file a certification with the Coast Guard Documentation Officer that the boat is properly *marked.* He must arrange for an official inspection of the marking if this is requested by the Coast Guard.

Every documented vessel, as a prerequisite to documentation, must have its official number and net tonnage carved or permanently marked on the *main beam* of the vessel.

The main beam is the beam at the forward end of the largest hatch on the weather deck and is usually located forward of amidships. If the vessel has no hatch on the weather deck, the main beam is any structural member integral to the hull.

### Official Number and Net Tonnage

The *official number* must be preceded by the abbreviation "NO." and the net tonnage must be preceded by the word "NET."

In a wooden vessel, the legend must be carved or cut on the main beam in arabic numbers and block type letters three inches high, or as high as the width of the main beam will permit. In a vessel built of metal, the legend must be outlined by punch marks and painted over with oil paint using a color that contrasts with the background.

On fiberglass boats, the legend can be carved into a plastic plate as in a wooden beam and this plate then is permanently bonded to a structural member integral to the hull or to the hull itself where one might expect to find a main beam. The plate will usually be six inches high and as long as necessary to show the required information.

All documented yachts are required to have their name and home port or hailing port marked on *some conspicuous place* on their hull; this is usually done on the stern. The letters must be Roman type and not less than four inches in height. They may be painted, gilded, cut, or cast letters, and must be in a color that has adequate contrast with the background.

## Name and Hailing Port

The *home port* is the port where the craft is permanently documented. The *hailing port* is the port or place in the same Marine Inspection Zone where the vessel was built or where one or more of the owners reside. The state name, in full or abbreviated form, should be included in the home or hailing port.

Documented commercial vessels must have the name and home or hailing port marked in full on the stern, plus the name in full marked on both bows.

For documented vessels, whether used for pleasure only or commercially, *the use of script or italic lettering is not acceptable.* It is *not* permissible to place the name or hailing port on a board and attach the board to the hull, or to use cut or carved letters joined in one continuous piece.

## Yacht Documents

If a vessel is given a document as a yacht, that paper will authorize its use for *pleasure only.* A yacht document does *not* permit the transporting of merchandise or the carrying of passengers for hire, such as the taking out of fishing parties for a fee charged directly or indirectly. Any violation of this limitation may result in the imposition of severe penalties against the craft and its owner.

The documentation of a vessel as a yacht *does not exempt* it from any applicable State or Federal taxes. Further, the fact that a boat is federally documented will not excuse the owner from complying with safety and equipment regulations of the state or states in which it is operated.

Vessels that are documented are not required nor permitted to have a number issued under the 1971 Federal Boat Safety Act. This saves state numbering fees.

## Document Renewal

A yacht license or enrollment and license must be renewed each year; this is probably the only disadvantage to documentation. The owner will ordinarily be notified by mail and will be sent the required renewal form and instructions several weeks in advance of the expiration date. Failure to receive this notice, however, will not affect the requirement for renewal.

At the discretion of the Officer in Charge, Marine Inspection, concerned, a document issued under the simplified measurement procedures *may* not be renewed, or another document issued, until the Coast Guard has verified the overall dimensions given in the application.

Any correction of the stated overall dimensions of a vessel as a result of the above verification is deemed to be a change in the description of the vessel and the outstanding document will no longer be in force.

# SHIP'S PAPERS/LICENSING

## STATE AND TERRITORIAL AGENCIES RESPONSIBLE FOR BOAT NUMBERING AND SAFETY LAWS

**State and Territorial Agencies**

**ALABAMA**
Marine Police Division
Department of Conservation & Natural Resources
State Administrative Building
Montgomery, Alabama 36130
Tel: Area Code 205: 832-6350

**ALASKA**
Alaska State Troopers
Department of Public Safety
P.O. Box 6188 Annex
Anchorage, Alaska 99502
Tel: Area Code 907: 264-5541

**ARIZONA**
Game & Fish Department
2222 West Greenway Road
Phoenix, Arizona 85023
Tel: Area Code 602: 942-3000

**ARKANSAS**
For Boat Registration:
Department of Finance & Administration
P.O. Box 1272 - Licensing Division
Little Rock, Arkansas 72201
Tel: Area Code 501: 371-1585
For Education & Enforcement:
Game & Fish Commission
#2 Natural Resources Drive
Little Rock, Arkansas 72205
Tel: Area Code 501: 224-4921

**CALIFORNIA**
For Boat Registration:
Department of Motor Vehicles
Vessel Registration Section
Post Office Box 780
Sacramento, California 95814
Attn: Manager
Vessel Registration Section
Tel: Area Code 916: 445-8685

**COLORADO**
Division of Parks & Outdoor Recreation
13787 So. Highway 85
Littleton, Colorado 80125
Attn: Boating Safety Coordinator
Tel: Area Code 303: 795-6954

**CONNECTICUT**
Department of Environmental Protection
Law Enforcement Unit
Room 247 - State Office Building
Hartford, Connecticut 06115
Chief of Law Enforcement
(Boating Administrator)
or,
Coordinator of Boating
Enforcement & Special Services
Tel: Area Code 203: 566-3978
566-7820

**DELAWARE**
Department of Natural Resources &
Environmental Control
Edward Tatnall Building
Legislative Ave. & William Penn St.
P.O. Box 1401
Dover, Delaware 19901
Attn: Boating Administrator
Tel: Area Code 302: 678-4431

**FLORIDA**
For Boat Titles, Registration and Information:
Department of Natural Resources
Crown Building
Tallahassee, Florida 32304
Attn: Chief
Bureau of Boat Registration
Tel: Area Code 904: 488-1195
For Law Enforcement and Education:
Department of Natural Resources
Crown Building
Tallahassee, Florida 32304
Attn: Director of Boating Safety
Tel: Area Code 904: 588-5957

**GEORGIA**
Department of Natural Resources
Room 714
Trinity-Washington Building
Atlanta, Georgia 30334
Attn: Chief of Education Section
Tel: Area Code 404: 656-3534

# SHIP'S PAPERS/LICENSING

## HAWAII
Harbors Division
Department of Transportation
79 S. Nimitz Highway
Honolulu, Hawaii 96813
Attn: Boating Staff Officer
Tel: Area Code 808: 548-2515 or 548-2516

## IDAHO
Department of Parks & Recreation
2177 Warm Springs Avenue
State House
Boise, Idaho 83720
Attn: Boating Safety Coordinator
Tel: Area Code 208: 384-2154

## ILLINOIS
Division of Law Enforcement
Conservation Department
600 N. Grand Avenue, West
Springfield, Illinois 62702
Tel: Area Code 217: 785-8401

## INDIANA
Law Enforcement Division
Department of Natural Resources
606 State Office Building
Indianapolis, Indiana 46204
Attn: Boating Safety Administrator
Tel: Area Code 317:232-4010
812: 526-5521

## IOWA
State Conservation Commission
Wallace Building
Des Moines, Iowa 50319
Attn: Superintendent of Waters Section
Tel: Area Code 515: 281-3449

## KANSAS
Forestry, Fish & Game Commission
R.R. #2, Box 54A
Pratt, Kansas 67124
Attn: Boating Safety Officer
Tel: Area Code 316: 672-5911 Ext. 106

## KENTUCKY
Division of Water Enforcement
Department of Transportation
114 West Clinton Street
Frankfort, Kentucky 40601
Attn: Director State Boating Law
Tel: Area Code 502: 564-3910

## LOUISIANA
Louisiana Department of Wildlife & Fisheries
Wildlife & Fisheries Building
Quail Drive
Baton Rouge, Louisiana 70808
Attn: State Boating Law Administrator
Tel: Area Code 504: 342-5868

## MAINE
For Boat Registration, Enforcement and Safety Programs:
Division of Recreational Safety & Registration
Watercraft Section
Department of Inland Fisheries & Wildlife
284 State Street
Augusta, Maine 04333
Tel: Area Code 207: 289-2766
For Public Access Information and
Uniform Waterway Marking System
Bureau of Parks and Recreation
Department of Conservation
Augusta, Maine 04333
Tel: Area Code 207: 289-3821

## MARYLAND
For Boat Titles, Registration and Information:
Department of Natural Resources
Tawes State Office Building
Taylor Avenue
Annapolis, Maryland 21404
Attn: Boat Titles and Registration
Tel: Area Code 301: 269-3211
For Law Enforcement and Education:
Natural Resources Police
Tawes State Office Building
Taylor Avenue
Annapolis, Maryland 21404
Attn: Superintendent
Tel: Area Code 301: 269-2240

## MASSACHUSETTS
Division of Marine & Recreational Vehicles
150 Causeway Street
Boston, Massachusetts 02114
Tel: Area Code 617: 727-3900

# SHIP'S PAPERS/LICENSING

## MICHIGAN

For Boat Registration and Titling:
Department of State
Bureau of Driver & Vehicle Services
7064 Crowner Drive
Lansing, Michigan 48918
Tel: Area Code 517: 332-1589
For Boating Regulations, Enforcement, Education and Safety:
Law Enforcement Division
Department of Natural Resources
Stevens T. Mason Building
Post Office Box 30028
Lansing, Michigan 48909
Attn: Boating Administrator
Marine Safety Section
Tel: Area Code 517: 373-1650
373-1230

## MINNESOTA

For Boat Registration:
License & Registration Center
Department of Natural Resources
625 North Robert Street
Saint Paul, Minnesota 55101
Attn: Supervisor
Tel: Area Code 612: 296-4507
For Boating Regulations, Education and Safety:
Department of Natural Resources
Box 46
Centennial Office Building
Saint Paul, Minnesota 55155
Attn: State Boating Law Administrator
Tel: Area Code 612: 296-3336

## MISSISSIPPI

Mississippi Department of Wildlife Conservation
Bureau of Fisheries & Wildlife
P.O. Box 451
Jackson, Mississippi 39205
Tel: Area Code 601: 354-7333

## MISSOURI

Department of Public Safety
Missouri State Water Patrol
Post Office Box 603
Jefferson City, Missouri 65101
Tel: Area Code 314: 751-3333

## MONTANA

For Boat Registration:
Registrar's Bureau
Motor Vehicle Division
Department of Justice
Deer Lodge, Montana 59722
Tel: Area Code 406: 846-1423
For Information about Boat Equipment Requirements & Rules of Operation:
Enforcement Division
Department of Fish & Game
1420 East 6
Helena, Montana 59601
Tel: Area Code 406: 449-2452

## NEBRASKA

State Game & Parks Commission
2200 North 33rd Street
Post Office Box 30370
Lincoln, Nebraska 68503
Attn: State Boating Law Administrator
Tel: Area Code 402: 464-0641

## NEVADA

Nevada Department of Wildlife
Division of Law Enforcement
Post Office Box 10678
Reno, Nevada 89520
Tel: Area Code 702: 784-6214

## NEW HAMPSHIRE

For Information about Boat and Outboard Motor Registration, Boat Equipment Requirements & Rules of Operation:
Division of Safety Services
Department of Safety
Hazen Drive
Concord, New Hampshire 03301
Tel: Area Code 603: 271-3336

## NEW JERSEY

Bureau of Marine Law Enforcement
Department of Environmental Protection
Box 1889
Trenton, New Jersey 08625
Tel: Area Code 609: 292-3406

## NEW MEXICO
Bureau of Boating Safety
Post Office Box 1147
Santa Fe, New Mexico 87503
Attn: Boating Administrator
Tel: Area Code 505: 827-2726

## NEW YORK
Marine & Recreational Vehicles
Agency Buillding No. 1
South Mall
Albany, New York 12238
Tel: Area Code 518: 474-0446

## NORTH CAROLINA
Division of Boating
Wildlife Resources Commission
Archdale Building
Raleigh, North Carolina 27611
Tel: Area Code 919: 733-3231

## NORTH DAKOTA
State Game & Fish Department
2121 Lovett Avenue
Bismark, North Dakota 58505
Tel: Area Code 701: 224-2180

## OHIO
Division of Watercraft
Department of Natural Resources
Fountain Square
Columbus, Ohio 43224
Tel: Area Code 614: 466-3686

## OKLAHOMA
For Boat Registration, Motor Licensing & Titling:
State Tax Commission
2501 North Lincoln
Oklahoma City, Oklahoma 73194
Attn: Boat & Motor License Div.
Tel: Area Code 405: 521-2437
For Educaton & Enforcement:
Department of Public Safety
Post Office Box 11415
Oklahoma City, Oklahoma 73111
Attn: Oklahoma Highway Patrol
Lake Patrol Division
Tel: Area Code 405: 424-4011 Ext. 283

## OREGON
State Marine Board
3000 Market Street, N.E., No. 505
Salem, Oregon 97310
Tel: Area Code 503: 378-8589

## PENNSYLVANIA
Pennsylvania Fish Commission
3532 Walnut Street
Post Office Box 1673
Harrisburg, Pennsylvania 17120
Attn: Bureau of Waterways & State Boating Law Administrator
Tel: Area Code 717: 787-2192

## RHODE ISLAND
Department of Environmental Management
Division of Boating Safety
Quonset Administration Building 7
Davisville, Rhode Island 02854
Tel: Area Code 401: 294-4521

## SOUTH CAROLINA
Division of Boating
Wildlife & Marine Resources Dept.
Post Office Box 12559
Charleston, South Carolina 29412
Tel: Area Code 803: 795-6350

## SOUTH DAKOTA
Department of Wildlife, Parks & Forestry
Anderson Building
Pierre, South Dakota 57501
Tel: Area Code 605: 773-4195

## TENNESSEE
Tennessee Wildlife Resources Agency
Post Office Box 40747
Ellington Agricultural Center
Nashville, Tennessee 37204
Tel: Area Code 615: 741-1431

## TEXAS
Parks & Wildlife Department
4200 Smith School Road
Austin, Texas 78744
Attn: Supervisor Water Safety
Tel: Area Code 512: 475-4823

## UTAH
Division of Parks & Recreation
1596 West North Temple Street
Salt Lake City, Utah 84116
Tel: Area Code 801: 533-4459

## VERMONT
Marine Division
Department of Public Safety
Montpelier, Vermont 05602
Tel: Area Code 802: 828-2105

# SHIP'S PAPERS/LICENSING

**VIRGINIA**
Commission of Game and Fisheries
Post Office Box 11104
Richmond, Virginia 23230
Tel: Area Code 804: 257-1000

**WASHINGTON**
State Parks & Recreation Commission
7150 Cleanwater Lane (KY-11)
Olympia, Washington 98504
Attn: State Boating Administrator
Tel: Area Code 206: 754-1253

**WEST VIRGINIA**
Law Enforcement Division
Department of Natural Resources
State Office Building
Charleston, West Virginia 25305
Tel: Area Code 304: 348-2783 or 348-2784

**WISCONSIN**
Bureau of Law Enforcement
Department of Natural Resources
Post Office Box 7921
Madison, Wisconsin 53707
Attn: Boating Law Administrator
Tel: Area Code 608: 266-0859

**WYOMING**
Game & Fish Department
Cheyenne, Wyoming 82202
Attn: Watercraft Officer
Tel: Area Code 307: 777-7604 777-7605

**DISTRICT OF COLUMBiA**
Metropolitan Police Department
Harbor Patrol
550 Water Street, S.W.
Washington, D.C. 20024
Tel: Area Code 202: 727-4582

**PUERTO RICO**
Maritime Department
Puerto Rico Ports Authority
GPO Box 2829
San Juan, Puerto Rico 00936
Tel: Area Code 809: 722-2409

**VIRGIN ISLANDS**
Department of Conservation
Lagoon Fishing Center
Estate Frydenhoj #86
St. Thomas, Virgin Islands 00801
Attn: Boating Law Administrator
Tel: Area Code 809: 775-0470

## United States Coast Guard

**UNITED STATES COAST GUARD HEADQUARTERS:**

Commandant
U.S. Coast Guard (G-C/TP22)
Washington, D.C. 20590

Chief
Office of Boating Safety
U.S. Coast Guard (G-B/TP42)
Washington, D. C. 20590
Tel: Area Code 202: 426-1088

Boating Safety Advisory Council
U.S. Coast Guard (G-BA)
Washington, D. C. 20590
Tel: Area Code 202: 426-1080

Boating Information Branch
Office of Boating Safety
U.S. Coast Guard (G-BA-2)
Washington, D.C. 20590
Tel: Area Code 202: 426-9716

Chief
State Liaison & Compliance Division
Office of Boating Safety
U.S. Coast Guard (G-BLC/TP42)
Washington, D.C. 20590
Tel: Area Code 202: 426-4176

Chief
Boating Technical Division
Office of Boating Safety
U.S. Coast Guard (G-BBT)
Washington, D.C. 20590
Tel: Area Code 202: 426-4127

Chief, Auxiliary & Education Division
Office of Boating Safety
U.S. Coast Guard (G-BAE)
Washington, D.C. 20590
Tel: Area Code 202: 426-1077

## Federal Agencies

Department of the Army
Office, Chief of Engineers,
Civil Works Recreation -
Resources Management Branch
DAEN-CWO-R
Washington, D.C. 20314